D1736637

A Boy Named Su

A Boy Named Su

stories from a journey into genderqueerness

Sumu Tasib

Independently published in the United States.

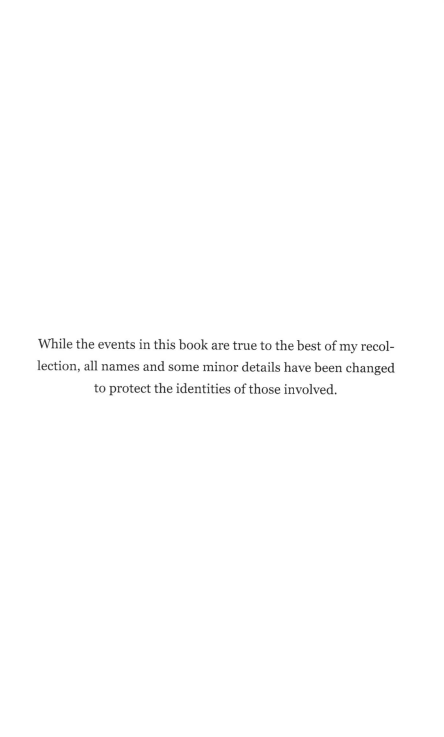

Contents

The Boy Who Fell to Earth

In the 1976 Nicolas Roeg film *The Man Who Fell to Earth*, David Bowie plays an interstellar traveler, Jerome Newton, who leaves his drought-ridden home planet seeking new sources of water, landing somewhere in the wilds of New Mexico. Though his spectacular sense of style and his uniquely Bowiean speech patterns would be enough to warn anyone he was not from around those parts, he manages to convince everyone he's from England, as though that would explain away all the eccentricities.

While his space-based inventions lead him quickly to fame and wealth, more than a few characters are drawn to our interstellar hero. While many seem perturbed, suspicious, or merely curious about his alien ways, the sprightly Mary-Lou is clearly attracted to him from their very first encounter, and before long the two are intimately involved. Over time, they move in together, and problems begin to surface. Mary-Lou is distraught at his standoffishness and Newton never seems to be completely comfortable around her. One night, in frustration, he peels off the costume of his human skin, revealing his alien form for the first time, and with a deep breath walks over to the bed and lays down alone.

Mary-Lou is utterly horrified, literally peeing in her underwear (the film was rated X when released in the US). However, she manages to pull herself together, takes off her clothes, and lays down with him, determined to make the relationship work. As she begins to slowly caress his alien body, she loses her nerve, screaming in disgust and fear as she runs out of the room.

It was when I saw that scene for the first time, in the midst of a global pandemic and quarantine, that I decided to write this book. I have been that person, pretending to be an ordinary boy, getting into an ordinary relationship, then one day out of frustration peeling back the costume to reveal myself as I really am, crawling into bed and holding my breath to see how my partner will react. I have berated myself for waiting that long, hoped against hope for openness and understanding, and feared most of all Mary-Lou's look of disgust and fear which would send me back into the shame spiral that drove me to hide myself in the first place.

In the waking world, I wear the costume of maleness easily and well; despite being non-white, and perhaps too eccentric to be seen as heteronormative, it doesn't take a sociologist to realize that there is a great deal of privilege and safety that comes with this life setting. Inside, though, things are far more complicated. Inside, there are elements of the feminine and the masculine, the stamen and the pistil, the water and the wind.

Beyond this, the movie made me realize I am far from alone in living this story. Indeed, if there are others out there on this journey, perhaps hearing my own experiences will help you make sense of your own. Perhaps my mistakes will help you learn to navigate the rougher waters; perhaps my moments of joy will remind you that there are flashes of beauty and love that make it all worthwhile.

Most importantly, for those of you who are struggling with the challenges of what it means to live in this human skin, I want you to know that you are not alone. If you get no further in this book, I want you to know that you are already "good enough," that you are valued, and that you are deserving of love. I recognize that this may seem like a radical notion, as it did to me when I first encountered it, and that in itself is a powerful statement as to how far we still have to go.

A Boy Named Su

Surgery

The intense pain must have started on a Friday night, but I don't remember the details; apparently my parents had rushed me to the ER and waited for hours only to be told it was "just a stomachache." As parents of a quiet seven-year old who had never cried in that way, they knew something more serious was going on, but the doctors reassured them it was nothing. I know it was a Friday only because I remember the following morning, resting on my parents' bed and watching cartoons. I was saying how I felt much better, and that my pediatrician, Dr. S, was a genius. He had said to drink 7-UP to calm my stomach, which I happily complied with, and now it was feeling tip-top. There was still a weird pain "lower down," though, I told them, and it wasn't going away. My mom had a worried look.

I was at our local clinic later that same afternoon, talking to Dr. S as I had so many times before. He was a kindly and caring man, greying at the temples, and I always felt comfortable in his presence, though behind his back we made good-natured fun of the perpetual smile he wore, whether he was saying "good morning" or "I'm going to give you a shot." At home, my sister and I would imitate him, jokingly saying things to each other like "I'm going to have to cut off your leg" or "I'm afraid this time it's your head" through our best facsimile of his tell-tale smile, doubling over in laughter as we made ever more preposterous and macabre proclamations. We always wondered whether there was any kind of news that would make him break that smile; to my dismay, I would learn the answer later that day.

After asking me some questions and palpitating various parts of my body, he looked right at me and said, "I'm afraid we're going to have to take you in to surgery." The smile was still there, but something in his face was not quite right. In my seven-year old mind, though, there were more important issues at hand. Without missing a beat, I asked, "Can I at least watch Sesame Street first?" In that moment Dr. S' smile disappeared completely. "I'm afraid not; we have to take you in right away."

The injustice of missing my favorite show somehow brought the gravity of the situation into focus, and I started crying uncontrollably. I remember crying all the way through the different stages of waiting rooms and pre-operative rooms with my mom trying desperately to console me. For years afterwards she would say that if she could have taken that pain instead of me she would have, and I wholly believe her; despite her flaws I will never forget the fierceness of the love she had for me. I remember the anesthesiologist holding my mask and firmly telling me to count down from ten and reassuring me despite my tears I would soon be asleep. That firm, confident voice from a larger-than-life figure towering over me remains one of my few clear memories of the operation; meeting him years later on a family walk I was shocked by his small stature and shy, retreating manner.

I woke up in a different body, one it would take me a while to understand. I remember a bright hospital room with a TV and an abundance of gifts – everyone we knew had sent toys and presents. Obsessed with miniature cars at the time, I was particularly thrilled to receive a Lotus "John Player Special" Formula One car, the fanciest toy car I had ever seen, from some family friends who had been visiting us when this all happened. I loved playing with that car while I was recovering, running it up and down the white hospital sheets covering my thin legs as I watched TV, but in my mind it became indelibly attached to the surgery. In later years it would give me a slightly sick feeling to see; I even shied away from playing with it, as though touching the car could take me right back to that hospital room.

I couldn't have been in the hospital for more than a few days, but in my memory it feels like weeks. I must have spent time recuperating at home, but that too I cannot recall. What I do remember are the scars, and the stitches. The first and most prominent scar was just below the curve of my belly, an angry, raised line from the near the center of my body tapering upwards towards my hip, crisscrossed with tough plastic threads that Dr. S. himself would painfully pull out about a month later. It was quite a few weeks before I noticed something else, a thin line of scabs down the center of my scrotum. Was that also from the surgery? Had I just injured myself? As a child who obsessively picked at scabs, I knew already it must have been around the same time, and very likely part of the procedure.

It was only then that I asked my mom what had actually happened, and she explained as best as she could. "You have two of these things, *sona,* they're under your *soosoo,* and one of them got all twisted up in itself and died, so they had to remove it." "But what about the other one?" I asked. "*Ishh,* You have to be extra careful with that one – don't sleep next to anyone, because they might kick you or get it twisted up and then you wouldn't be able to have any *bachha* of your own." I was terrified, not so much at the prospect of not having children, but that something in my body could just get twisted up and die – what would prevent this from happening again? What else in my body might suddenly die? For most of my childhood

Surgery

I was exceedingly careful when washing, dressing, and especially sleeping, worried that the slightest turn in bed could result in another surgery. I couldn't remember details about the procedure, but I knew I wanted to avoid a repeat experience at all costs.

For a few months my parents dragged me to various lawyers' offices to see if we could sue the E.R. doctor for missing the root cause; I came to learn that if he had acknowledged the location and extreme level of pain I was feeling and done the standard tests, it would have been obvious it wasn't a stomachache and he could have saved the testicle. In my mind, though, given the explanation from my mom, it was probably my fault for twisting around too much in bed. I worried the longer we talked to these fast-talking, inquisitive men in fancy wood-paneled offices, the sooner one of them would figure out it was nobody's fault but my own and convict me of self-inflicted injury in front of my horrified parents. When instead lawyer after lawyer said that there wouldn't be much of a case, my parents seething with frustration at a system they couldn't afford to navigate, I was secretly relieved that we were one step closer to putting all this behind us.

At home, in my room, other changes were happening that I couldn't understand. Somehow the operation must have triggered some aspects of sexual development much earlier than normal, and by age eight I was experiencing powerful and bewildering erections on a regular basis. I had no idea what was happening; I was certain it was a byproduct of the operation. I was too frightened to discuss it with my parents, as it would surely be evidence that I had continued to be careless while sleeping and caused additional damage. I found that if I rubbed my erections against my comforter it would feel good, and if I lay very, very still they would eventually subside. My sister once walked in on me doing this and complained to my mom that I was rubbing myself on my bed with the door open. I had never thought of my body as shameful before, but instantly I was deeply embarrassed, and soon after my parents installed locks for both of our doors without saying a word about what had happened.

In our conservative midwestern school district, I was still years away from any kind of meaningful sex education, but within a couple of years boys started talking about sex-related things on our own. My best friend Kenny walked in on his parents having sex and became something of a local celebrity as we all hounded him for details. He drew a picture to explain what was happening: his mother's vulva was in the center of her abdomen, his father's penis extended at a perfect ninety-degree angle from his body at the same height. The mechanics of this seemed entirely plausible to my ten year-old mind, so rather than doubt the picture, I doubted my own body.

Surgery

My erections, of course, did not point out at a ninety-degree angle, but instead aimed stubbornly towards the sky – clearly something was very wrong, likely because of the surgery. I had recently learned to sew from my mom, and now I put my piano bag and Barbie outfit projects aside to put those skills towards a much more urgent task: designing elaborate straps that would pull my erect penis down to the "correct" angle. I put these on and tied myself painfully tight anytime I felt an erection coming on, hoping to "train" my penis into normalcy.

I eventually got past these initial concerns as I learned more about how bodies were supposed to work, and began to worry more about how the absence of a testicle might affect my development. Dr. S. assured me that this wouldn't be a problem, that my remaining testicle would grow in size and be able to take on the work of both. To this day, though, I wonder how the surgery affected my sexual development and gendered characteristics. Having become a scientist in my professional life, I cannot help but occasionally scour the literature to see what is known about the effects of losing a testicle on secondary sex characteristics, testosterone, gender identity, or orientation; the answers are few and far between.

For whatever reason, I was never concerned about how my lovers would react to my single testicle, but I continued to be worried about the risks of losing the other one to an unconscious kick from a sleeping bedmate. A year or so before I met my first lover, I woke up one morning with a dull pain in my scrotum. Fearing the worst, I rushed to my graduate school's medical center, which was conveniently located right next to my lab. I was frantically explaining the pain I was feeling and that I was afraid of losing the other testicle, while the doctor stayed irritatingly calm.

"Well it looks like they left part of the epididymis in the testicle they removed, I'm not sure why, and it appears to be a little inflamed, no big deal," he said authoritatively.

"Well I'm glad it's no big deal to you, but I'm just a little concerned that the other one's going to get all twisted up and then I'll lose that one too!" I blurted out.

He looked over at me and narrowed his eyes a bit, "Have you ever read the operative note?"

"The what?" I asked.

"The operative note – the detailed notes from your operation," he explained. "In most cases when a testicle undergoes a torsion, they suture the other one to the scrotal wall to prevent a second torsion."

This caught me unawares; I had never thought to even ask about such a thing. I immediately called my childhood hospital and asked that the operative note be faxed to the health center. A few days later, I read it in the doctor's office, for the first time seeing the details of what happened. The flawed connection of the epididymis creating a weak point, the diagnosis of the torsion, the onset of gangrene (a result of the delay and thus the rush to surgery), the location of the incisions, the removal of the dead organ, and finally, "remaining testicle sutured to scrotal wall." I breathed a huge sigh of relief; at least that was one aspect of my yet-to-begin sex life that I could stop worrying about. He then asked if I'd ever considered getting a prosthetic to replace my lost testicle. Still coming down from the relief of learning about the suture, I laughed.

"Why? What would it do?" I asked.

"Well, nothing," he said hurriedly, a little embarrassed, "just for a sense of, you know, symmetry..."

I laughed again. "So you're suggesting a highly invasive surgical procedure for the sake of *symmetry?*"

"Okay never mind then," he said gruffly and turned back to his notes.

Speaking as someone who has had their scrotum cut open once, trust me when I tell you it's not something one would do again willingly.

It does make me reflect on why he would have suggested a course of action that even today seems so absurd to me. To him, as with many men, having two testicles was a fundamental part of being a man. I only fully realized this decades later when consoling a friend who was about to lose a testicle to cancer; while I was blathering on about practicalities like how it wouldn't affect sexual function, he was inconsolable, and I eventually realized he was grieving the loss of his perceived manhood.

Having grown up with only one, I had never even considered this perspective. I now think about the societal cues we have all around us, from "truck nuts" to the everyday expressions we have around testicles – "you don't have the *balls* for that," "grow a *pair*," or "that's a *ballsy* move" – always plural. A single (or small) testicle, on the other hand, is grounds for ridicule and mockery, as in the World War II era British song "Hitler Has Only Got One Ball." According to the society's rules, if you don't have two spongy masses (and preferably large ones) in a sack of skin hanging from your groin, you're not a "real man" – perfectly fine by me.

Fortunately, I grew up without anyone outside my family knowing about my unique anatomy, and as such I was never subjected to teasing on that basis. As the years have gone on I've become increasingly comfortable talking about that aspect of my body; it has never been something I've felt shame about – odd, in a way, given how I've felt about so many other things about my sexuality. I've joked that if I were an electronic music artist my moniker would be "DJ Monotesticular," and once when I and a friend (who had the same affliction, different testicle) were both dating the same woman, I liked to joke that individually each of us was only *half* a man, but between the two of us we made up a whole boyfriend. "That's not funny," he would say, trying not to laugh; "you're right," I'd return, "it's hilarious! I'm having a *ball*, aren't you?" I've even giggled when a new lover first puts her hand down there, freezing and then fumbling around after feeling only one, waiting a tense moment before I reveal my anatomical secrets.

These days the question I always come back to is how the surgery affected the development of my body and mind. Maleness and masculinity have always felt foreign to me; I can feign them when necessary, but I've always recognized it as an act. In terms of secondary sex characteristics, while most of the men in my family are exceedingly hairy, I have almost no body hair at all (beyond my head), and I couldn't grow a full moustache if I wanted to (I don't). I've been told by past lovers, sometimes with a hint of jealousy, that my skin is exceedingly soft, especially for a man. The default register of my voice is unexpectedly high; on the phone I've often been mistaken for a woman. Overshadowing all of this, though, are my feelings of gender identity, the topic of this book. Could some or all of this have been a consequence of the surgery?

I will probably never know, but I also will probably never stop thinking about it. For as long as I can remember, I have been obsessed with the cause behind the effect: even in those cartoons I watched from my parents' bed I had to know how Batman became the way he was, what motivated the "bad guys" to be bad, how Superman figured out he could fly. It's followed me right into my adulthood and led to my career as a scientist; I am constantly digging deeper to understand the "why" behind the "what." It's no wonder, then, upon finally accepting myself as I am, I can't help but want to know where it all began.

Bean Bags and Benches

One of my favorite things as a kid was to be sick. Not so sick that I couldn't read a book or watch TV, but just sick enough that I'd be guaranteed to be able to stay home for a few days. I had even come up with an optimal temperature: 102.5 degrees. That would mean at least staying home that day, very likely still being sick the next day, and then the extra day at home "just to make sure" that my Mom always insisted on. If it was Wednesday (the best day to get sick), the weekend would be tacked on, and I could spend five blissful days at home. All of this was not because I disliked school – on the contrary, I rather enjoyed it most of the time – it was more about spending one-on-one time with my mom. Though she was often volatile, even violent, in the context of the whole family, when it was just the two of us, and especially when I was sick, she was exceptionally tender and loving. I craved that time and the rare warmth of that love.

A Boy Named Su

As a result, I came up with all kinds of crazy schemes to get myself sick. At a very young age, my mom told us never to go to bed with our pajama tops wet, since that would make you sick for sure – guess who went to sleep most nights with an uncomfortably wet pajama top. She said to always wear a hat during the winter, since if we didn't we'd catch a cold immediately, so as soon as I was out of sight, I'd take it off; again, not to look cool, but to maximize my chances of getting sick.

As I got to be ten or so, I was learning more about science, and came up with more elaborate schemes. Our family's ancient glass thermometer with its three-minute sand timer was the ultimate arbiter of whether we could stay home: it had to be above 100 to guarantee time with Mom. I developed a theory that since the timer was for a precise period of three minutes, and required shaking the thermometer down to its baseline 94 degrees before starting a measurement, it was probably not showing the equilibrium temperature in the body, but rather was calibrated based on how much the actual body temperature would move the mercury within the specified time period. If this were true, then holding the thermometer in longer than the prescribed period would result in a higher temperature – and it worked! It didn't move things that much, but I could often get 99 degrees to cross that coveted 100 degree threshold. Eventually my Mom caught on to my scheme, but I had a few years of slightly inflated temperatures to keep me home at least once a month. My parents would talk worriedly about how I was growing up to be a sickly child, while I would be gleefully huddled in a blanket and watching cartoons.

In the endless quest for that just-high-enough fever, I carefully read the instructions for the thermometer, and one day noticed that rectal temperatures were typically a full degree higher than oral. I was a little concerned about putting a thin stick of glass into my bottom, but for the greater good of staying home with Mom it was worth a try. I followed the instructions to the letter, using a small amount of petroleum jelly applied to the tip. While the temperature rise wasn't quite as dramatic as I had hoped, I discovered something else – the cool metal tip of the thermometer felt surprisingly good inside me. Soon I started experimenting with putting more and more of the shaft inside myself, coating the whole of the glass housing with petroleum jelly, until the entire crayon-sized thermometer was inside me. At this point, being a cautious child (and with an early interest in chemistry), I began to worry about the possibility of the glass breaking and leaking toxic mercury into my body, and looked for other objects I could play with more safely in the same way.

In those early days, I tried just about everything – vegetables (carefully wrapped afterwards in paper towels and thrown away to hide the evidence), wadded up toilet paper, trial-size bottles of shampoo, ice cubes (a painful disaster), even a panic-inducing experience with a rubber superball that went in easily but didn't want to come back out. Unfortunately, I found nothing that could match the pleasure of the cool, smooth glass of the thermometer. Some of these experiences would induce powerful erections, though I was still years away from my first orgasm. Having read a little bit about sexual function at this time, I thought the pre-cum that always came with these adventures was semen, despite not matching what I'd read in terms of color, consistency, or volume. Like most deviations from my naïve notion of sexual norms, I chalked this up to the surgery.

Around the same time, my knees started giving me a lot of trouble. I was a small child and hardly athletic, and as our parents constantly warned us of the horrific injuries that could be caused by climbing trees, riding bikes, etc., I mostly stayed indoors and had my adventures in storybooks. We took our concerns to Dr. S., and in his usual smiling way he recommended weight-bearing exercises, specifically seated leg-extensions, in which one sits on the edge of a bench with the shins behind foam pads, lifting the weight out and up, as well as leg curls, in which one lies on their stomach and puts their heels below the bar, pulling the weights towards themselves.

We had very little money at the time but managed to find a used weight bench with a leg extension unit as well as a set of blue plastic sand-filled weights in the classifieds; we set it up in the basement near the TV. Early on, I just did the leg extensions, and though I found them dull they seemed to be helping my knees a little bit. Once I moved on to the leg curls, I discovered something unexpected. The bar I put my heels behind for the curl, attached to the hinge at one edge of the bench, extended its hard, cool, 1" diameter steel tubing about six inches beyond the bar, ending in a smooth, rounded cap, presumably so that one could easily slip additional weights over the end.

Probably the very first time I did that exercise, fully clothed, I felt the tip of that bar push up against my bottom. Before long I was waiting until everybody was out of the house, taking off all my clothes, and just letting that tip touch me. It was electrifying. I soon learned if I turned over onto my back, I could hold the bar with my hands, and have a great deal of control over where and how hard it pressed up against my bottom.

At that time, I had not had anything nearly that large inside me, and I doubted that it would even be possible. Still, I wanted to try, so whenever I was alone in the house, I would wrap the shaft in saran wrap, apply a generous amount of hand lotion (I had graduated from petroleum jelly), and spend blissful moments just pushing it up against me. Eventually, with patience, perseverance, and a little bit of pain, I was able to get the tip inside me, and to my surprise found that the rest of the shaft followed smoothly and with little effort into my eager bottom, all the way to the hilt, with the crossbar pressed up against my cheeks.

This was a wholly new sensation – to feel completely filled, to be able to squeeze down on the shaft with the entirety of my body, to slowly slide it in and out as I did so. Despite not being able to orgasm, and not even touching myself (both hands were on the bar controlling the shaft), it was a feeling of electrifying bliss. Over time, I became more and more reckless with when I would play with it, no longer being extra careful that everybody would be out of the house for hours. There was one time when I had worked the shaft all the way to the hilt, sighing with pleasure, when I heard car doors slam in the garage and the kitchen door opening – a mere 11 steps away from being able to see me. I was completely naked, with six inches of metal shaft all the way inside me, and I knew I had to move *fast*. I pushed against the bar to (painfully) free myself of the shaft, dove for my clothes, and ripped the saran wrap off and into my pocket. I was only moments ahead of my dad coming down the stairs to find out what the commotion was. It was a close call, and my bottom was sore for a few days; I was much more careful after that.

As the years went on, I spent a lot more time with that shaft inside me than I did working out; fortunately my knees seemed to get better on their own. Over time, though, I became increasingly focused on the feeling of my erection, and not yet knowing what to do with that, I just rubbed myself against things. With very little knowledge or guidance on sex available to me from my usual go-tos (the 60s-era family *Encyclopædia Brittanica* and the public library's card catalog), I tried a little bit of everything – couches, bedspreads, shag carpets, a soapy bathtub, you name it.

The object that felt particularly good, though, was a large yellow bean bag we had in the basement. It was big enough to support my entire body, but if I mounted it just so, I could reach the ground with my toes, and slide my body against a groove that would naturally appear in the vinyl. For months this resulted in the pre-cum I was used to, and I thought I had a pretty good handle on what sex was, though it wasn't quite as dramatic as I had imagined it to be.

Then, one unexpected afternoon, in the midst of my usual thrusting, it suddenly felt like my legs took on a mind of their own, the muscles contracting rapidly of their own accord. I was moving faster and faster against the bean bag and suddenly, almost in slow motion, I experienced the first, explosive orgasm of my young life. Based on the volume and consistency, I quickly realized that this was the first time I had genuinely achieved an orgasm, and I was breathless with excitement. This was a level of pleasure I had never experienced before, and in a moment all my energies became directed towards recreating that experience.

I cleaned things up that day and tried many, many times to replicate that first shuddering release, but never achieved it again with the yellow bean bag. Instead I came up with a woefully inefficient (and painful) method to manually achieve orgasm: I simulated the bean bag's vinyl groove by cupping my hand over my shaft, then rubbing vigorously until I came. Burn marks and scars were common as I began to do this as often as my body would support (every twenty minutes or so), and I would get head-splitting "orgasm hangovers" I learned to live with for some months afterwards. I never mixed the two – while I loved the feeling of having things in my bottom, and I also loved the feeling of ejaculation, I never tried stimulating my butt while masturbating. In my mind they were just separate things that gave me a great deal of pleasure; one I could do any time in my room, clutching my favorite stuffed panda bear in my other arm, and one that required everyone to be out of the house. Furthermore, given the choice, I would always opt for the intensity of an orgasm, so my more adventurous forms of butt play faded further and further into the background as traditional masturbation took center stage.

By age eleven, my classmates and I were far enough along in puberty to start talking about it, and I began to learn about the strict binary categories of heterosexual (penis-in-vagina) and homosexual (penis-in-anus) sex and sexual orientation. There were childish theories about whether the person with the penis vs. the person with the anus were "equally gay," but there was no question that the latter was "totally gay." As such, I couldn't help but wonder if that was the case with me; I very much enjoyed having things in my butt, and even the thought of it would give me secret pleasure while bored in class. However, I had no attraction whatsoever to other boys. I had been drawn to girls from before the first grade, and my attractions grew more intense with every year. When masturbating I would only think about girls; I would try thinking about boys to see what would happen but even the thought would quickly dampen my erections. Despite the stigma against being gay, this made me even more anxious, since at least if I were attracted to boys I could fit neatly into the established binary.

The next few years of middle school and high school did little to clarify things – all I knew was that I was not like the others. I told no one of my anal pleasures, and tried half-heartedly to be assertive, artificially lower my voice, and date a couple of women as a "regular guy," but those dates filled me more with anxiety than joy. My shy and soft manner had little to offer to my conservative midwestern classmates, and when those "relationships" ended I was generally more relieved than sad, happy to be back in my world of fantasy.

Alone in my room, I would squeeze my eyes tight and masturbate vigorously, at first to images in my mind, then to women singers on the radio, and eventually over lingerie ads I'd secretly clipped from European fashion magazines. My parents were somewhat perplexed at the stacks of magazines I would bring home from the library, chalking it up to an unusual interest in fashion. While at the time I thought I was clever for fooling them, in retrospect perhaps my interest in clothing and style began with the immaculately dressed women and men on those shiny pages. I perfected a technique of slicing out individual pages without leaving a mark, and had a green cardboard folder I kept all the clippings in, unlikely to be found among my ever-growing collection of school materials. That folder traveled with me to college and played its part in my fantasies until the end of my undergraduate days.

When I dreamed of romance, though, my thoughts went elsewhere. I pored over J. Crew catalogs, the blue-eyed women in oversized cable-knit sweaters lounging by a fire in a soft-toned New England cabin, their square-jawed boyfriends coming in from an afternoon of rugby to confidently put an arm around them on the couch. How I wished for that kind of casual intimacy, that confident masculinity, that soft and idyllic beauty. Looking in the mirror, though, it felt completely out of reach, nothing that a pricey Irish Fisherman-style sweater would be able to solve, even if I were able to afford it.

I was completely fascinated by women, their faces, their voices, their bodies, their clothes, but had no idea how to approach them, let alone be fully present with them. I would constantly hear the advice to "be myself," but I was quite certain that if I revealed myself as I really was, no sane woman would even want to be in the same room as me. As such, I mostly put off the question of dating until college, not because I expected my understanding of women to change, but in the hopes that a sufficiently different (and more liberal) population might find other aspects of me interesting enough to overlook the strangeness of my manners and desires.

The future would prove to be substantially more complicated than that, and I wonder whether the journey might have been simpler had I heeded that clichéd advice back in my midwestern youth. I was not so naïve even then, though, to not recognize such revelations could have ended in violence or even death. Men who were even suspected of not being entirely heterosexual were harassed mercilessly in my hometown; I had enough bullying to fend off given my tiny stature and bookish nature. Out of an early instinct for safety, I never mentioned anything about my secret pleasures to a soul in my hometown. In fact, it would be almost a decade later before I would reveal them to anyone.

There was a part of me that desperately wanted to share what was inside me, to understand what it meant, but I had made my decision: I was going to Cambridge, Massachusetts, where I would find my one true blue-eyed J. Crew love, and this silly anal fixation would just be a funny childhood story that we'd laugh at someday, preferably over a glass of dark red wine, as we relaxed by the fire in a soft-toned New England cabin.

Ghost

There's a letter on the desktop
That I dug out of a drawer
The last truth we ever came to
In our adolescent war

And I start to feel the fever
Like the warm air through the screen
You come regular like seasons
Shadowing my dreams...

--"Ghost", The Indigo Girls

It was the spring of my sophomore year in college, and I was lying in bed in a tiny single dorm room with a fever of 103.5, nearly delirious. I was a full degree over the "optimal temperature" of my youth, my mom was thousands of miles away, and there was no longer any joy at all in being sick. In the midst of that haze, I listened intently to the lyrics from this song from the Indigo Girls, track three on a free sampler CD I'd picked up from the Student Center. I set it on repeat so I could listen to it over and over and over again, thinking about Sahila.

Sahila was my first and longest crush in college; I met her in the very first week of my first year, our so-called "orientation week," days before classes even started. A group of us had gone to check out a party off campus in Kenmore Square, and amongst other friends there was this quiet, pensive woman in an oversized men's blazer, a stylishly boyish haircut, deep serious eyes, and even more serious and expressive eyebrows. She would stop sometimes while speaking, mid-sentence, seeming to freeze, her eyes flickering and looking troubled; her friends would just ignore her and keep talking, but I was fascinated – I wanted to know what was going on behind the dark pools of her eyes. It was a face and a personality I would not soon forget.

A few months after that first meeting, still adjusting to the intensity of my classes and living with two unfriendly roommates in a single room, I had a new crush. Nancy, lovely Nancy, born and bred in New England, lived in the room right next door. She was a classical J. Crew beauty with grey-blue eyes and long chestnut hair that fit all the visions of my child-hood dreams. I soon learned I was not the only one who felt this way: she fast became the love interest of at least four other dorm-mates, perhaps all of whom had grown up with the same soft-toned catalogs. Over time Nancy and I would form a close friendship which would long outlast the crush, but those days were yet to come. At this point, all I could think about was her, and one day she unexpectedly cornered me into revealing who I had a crush on. Not wanting to reveal the truth, I attempted to divert the conversation by mentioning the only other woman who had made a lasting impression on me.

"There's this woman, Sahila, who I met during orientation week," I said cautiously.

"Wait," Nancy said, "Sahila Sarkar? Is she a tennis player? She's in my chemistry class!" she said, getting excited.

"I don't know," I responded, alarmed at the direction this was taking.

She asked me to describe her, and it quickly became clear we were talking about the same person. "I can totally introduce you to her," she said with a mischievous glint in her eyes.

At this point I honestly wasn't even sure that I was interested in Sahila, but Nancy had become so excited I played along. We planned an elaborate scheme where she would schedule a lunch with her friend in the Student Center cafeteria; I would just happen to run into Nancy in the food area, and she would invite me to join them at their table.

The day arrived and I was mostly excited about spending time with Nancy, but when I was gathering my food and soda onto my gray plastic tray I came around a corner to come face-to-face with Sahila. We both froze at the unexpected encounter; I had rarely seen her in the months since orientation week, and when I had it was only from afar. Suddenly I was looking directly into her eyes and lost all sense of where I was. The only thing that snapped me out of it was a rapid motion in my peripheral vision as my full soda cup accelerated towards the edge of the tray. In a moment of extraordinary luck and coordination, I managed to tip the tray up just in time without spilling anything. When I looked up again, Sahila was gone, on her way to find Nancy in the dining area.

The ruse worked as planned and I sat down with them for lunch. I hardly said anything, but I hung on Sahila's every word. I can't remember what she talked about, but her face, her expressions, her rapid and halting manner of speech were all burning into my memory. My eyes went back and forth between Nancy and Sahila, and despite Nancy being the J. Crew ideal of my youth, despite our having a close rapport over countless conversations in our dorm, I couldn't take my eyes and ears off of Sahila.

Ghost

I never did ask her out after that introductory lunch, or any-time during that first year of college, and as weeks became months and months became years, other crushes came and went, but I always came back to Sahila. Sometime in my sophomore year I remember telling a male friend about this obsession, and he responded with a look of disgust – "Sahila? Why do you like *her*? She looks like a *dude*." I remember lashing out angrily at him in response.

A few months later, though, I saw what I thought was my friend Manny coming up to greet me at a dorm party wearing his ubiquitous backwards baseball cap. I gave him a huge smile and "Heyyyyy" as he was one of my favorite people, only to realize as he (no, she!) broke into a huge smile that it was not Manny at all, but Sahila. At that point I had to admit to myself that there were in fact masculine elements to her aesthetic: her strong jaw, her athletic movements, her smirk-like smile. To my surprise, this made me no less attracted to her; in some ways it drew me to her even more. Though I would sometimes get close to other women, the thought of Sahila always pulled me back, and I ended up not dating at all throughout my undergraduate years.

Over the years there were several times we would almost end up on a date together, but it never quite happened. For a while she was dating a much older man, and shortly after that fell apart I ran into her outside her dorm desperately looking in all directions. "Hey Su," she pleaded, "Want to go to brunch with me?" It turned out her friends had unexpectedly left without her, leaving me with a perfect opportunity, but I was too terrified and told her I had to study.

In the early weeks of our senior year, she called me up out of the blue to see if I wanted to see Sarah McLachlan with her and help her get tickets for her friends. As I was also a big fan (though I would have gone with her regardless), I joined her on a winter morning at 8am, fourth and fifth in line in front of Tower Records on Newbury Street. We were there about an hour before the store opened; this was the longest we had ever spent alone together. We talked awkwardly, learning more about each other, as I tried my best to hide both how cold I felt and how incredibly nervous I was. Suddenly I felt dizzy and almost fainted, dropping to one knee on the ground. Sahila caught my arm and asked if I was ok. I told her I felt faint and she insisted on going to a coffeeshop with me and getting me some food.

"I think it was just the cold and not having eaten anything," I said.

She looked at me, worried, and said, "You should definitely get checked out just to make sure nothing is wrong."

She was a pre-med student, and I trusted her judgment. We got back in line and got the tickets, and I made a quick trip to the campus medical center on the way home as she had recommended.

"There's nothing wrong with you," the doctor chuckled, "but it sounds like you really have a thing for this young lady."

Our senior year ended quickly, a blur of parties, bars, speeches, ceremonies, and goodbyes. Sahila and I saw each other surprisingly often during this time, mostly by virtue of being in all the same student groups and thus invited to all the same events. We would always seek each other out, talking and laughing like old friends in these last days together. She left for home for the summer and would go to the Midwest for medical school in the fall. I was staying in Cambridge for graduate school and started working in my lab-to-be as soon as graduation was over. I felt a certain relief at her finally leaving town – perhaps I could now start dating someone without constantly thinking about the possibility of things working out with Sahila.

Within weeks of her departure, I had started hanging out with Koko, another tennis player, and during our first walk together over the Harvard bridge our hands started touching and almost without thinking our fingers intertwined. That first hand-holding escalated quickly to a first kiss, and within days we were stealing up to her room for dinner and passionate make-out sessions. We were becoming more daring with our mouths and hands with every encounter, though in our innocence we never made it past each others' underwear, and would go home each night to our solitary beds.

For a few weeks, I felt like I had overcome the awkwardness of my high school years as well as my undergraduate obsession, and could now start a series of healthy relationships. There were hints of Sahila that kept appearing, but I mostly managed to keep them at bay. One slip occurred near Koko's birthday, when I had decided to get her some perfume. Not knowing much about different scents, and having once heard from Sahila that she used White Musk from the Body Shop, I thought that this might be perfect for Koko as well, naively thinking I liked the fragrance rather than its association with my crush.

I went to the store at the Prudential Mall to test it out. The salesperson put a bit on my skin and I sniffed it; it seemed nothing at all like I remembered. I bought it anyway, thinking the scent might be different on a woman's skin. As I walked out of the mall and crossed the street, wondering why I had bothered to waste money on what was very likely the wrong perfume, the scent began to comingle with my skin and permeate the air around me. Suddenly I felt the familiar notes bringing back a flood of memories and I stopped in the middle of the street, looking all around for her, only then realizing what had happened. Of course I should have known better than to try this, but at least I had the good sense to not give that bottle to Koko.

At the height of summer, I received a call in my graduate dorm room from Sahila. "I'm coming to town for a few days, do you want to hang out? There's something I need to tell you." In an instant everything came back, and I could think about nothing but Sahila. Immediately I realized that as much I was enjoying my time with Koko, she never evoked this intensity of feeling, and I had to let my first real girlfriend go. I broke up with her awkwardly and painfully, over the course of two nights – when she cried in my arms the first night it was the first time I had ever been the cause of someone else's heartbreak, and naively wanting to put a stop to that pain I promised her we could keep trying. My mind had not changed, though, and a few nights later I ended it for good, which understandably made her incredibly angry. I am not at all proud of how I behaved – I gave her no meaningful explanation, and to this day I regret the hurt I caused. I wish I could have been kinder, but at that moment I was too obsessed with a ghost to think about anything else.

A week later Sahila arrived, staying in a friend's room at her old dorm, seeing friends for a few days; she had saved the last night she was in town for us to meet up for dinner. Afterwards, we walked home from Central Square, and she asked if we could get some alcohol before our talk. "Of course," I said, wondering what might be coming, and we bought some cheap beer at a convenience store. As we walked down Massachusetts Avenue to her room, she stopped to point up at the moon, walking back and forth on the sidewalk to get the best vantage point.

"Wow," she said, "Look at the moon! It's incredible!"

I agreed, wondering why she was stalling in this way. Nervous as I was, I said little; fortunately the night was warm and the dangers of fainting were low. Eventually we got to her room, sat down next to each other, and started to talk.

"Well what is it you wanted to talk to me about?" I asked, at least as nervous as she seemed to be.

"Uh..., let's drink first," she said, stalling again.

She had a much higher tolerance than me, and two beers in I was on the edge of being drunk.

"OK, here it is," she said, and then paused in her halting way.

In that moment, my mind was whirling with the possibilities. Was she finally going to tell me she had feelings for me as well? Did she want to sleep with me on this last chance we had together? Was she going to tell me about a new man she was dating?

Ghost

After the last swig of her third beer, she started to speak again. "So this summer I met this woman."

"Oh?" I responded quizzically, not sure where this was going.

"Yeah, I mean, I didn't know what it was at first, but then we got closer and closer, and before long we were making out, and then dating, it just felt *so right*, you know?"

"Oh wow!" I replied, not knowing what else to say.

I was stunned. A flood of feelings had overtaken me – surprise, of course, but also an incredible sense of release, and the freedom I thought I had felt when she first left town, much more real this time. While I would have been jealous of any man and continued to pine after her, obviously I couldn't compete with any woman, so I could finally be free from my obsession. Sensing all the anxiety I had been feeling melt away, I asked her to tell me everything about her new love. We had a wonderful conversation, she told me about her parents' skepticism about the relationship and how much she appreciated my acceptance. We left that night closer than we had ever been, and I felt happier and freer than I had in a long time.

The next time I heard from her was a late November evening a year into my doctoral program; she had called me at the office after trying me at home.

"What are you doing right now?" she asked.

Thinking she might be suddenly in town, I said, "Nothing, what's up?"

"Have you heard of Ani DiFranco?" she asked.

"I've heard the name but I don't know her music," I replied.

"Ok," she said, "I want you to go down to the Orpheum right now, she's playing at 7:30 tonight. You *need* to hear her music."

"But it's almost 7!" I protested.

"Then leave now," she said. "Hurry."

The urgency in her voice and my long connection with her made me powerless to resist. I hopped on the T and made it to the dark alley that was the entrance to the concert hall just after 7:45; nobody was left outside.

I walked up to the bored-looking ticket agent and asked if I could get a ticket. Rolling her eyes she said "sold out" flatly through the microphone, pointing at a huge lit-up signboard that had the same message. "Thanks," I said, waiting in the alley for a while to see if I could hear the music that Sahila wanted me so urgently to absorb.

I couldn't hear a thing, so I went to the same Tower Records where we'd once waited for tickets together and picked up a copy of Ani's latest CD, *Not a Pretty Girl*. I went back to the lab, put it in my Discman, and started listening. From the first folk-punk bars of "Cradle and All" it was clear this was music I would fall in love with, and over the years I've become only more enamored with that album. Even back then, though, when I understood so little about my gender identity, the words of "32 Flavors" were strangely resonant:

> *I am a poster girl with no poster*
> *I am thirty-two flavors and then some*
> *And I'm beyond your peripheral vision*
> *So you might wanna turn your head*
> *'Cause someday you're gonna be starving*
> *And eating all of the words you just...said*

Some years later she called me again out of the blue; this time to tell me her identical twin sister Sanila was going to do a residency in Boston, and since she didn't know anyone there, she was asking if I could show her around. I told her I'd be happy to, and initially my motivations were pure; I just wanted to help out my friend's sister. As we spent a few evenings together, though, despite her personality and mannerisms being quite different, her face so reminded me of Sahila's that I found myself becoming more and more attracted to her. One night crossing the same bridge over which Koko and I had first held hands, I reached for Sanila's, and she gently pushed it away.

"I'm flattered," she said, "but I know how you felt about my sister, and I feel like you might be interested in me for the wrong reasons."

"No," I said defensively, feeling the blood rush to my face, "it's not that at all, I know you're a completely different person."

No more hand-holding occurred that night, and after a few more evenings, I realized she was right – while her face reminded me of that ghost from the past, I never felt drawn to Sanila in the way I had with her sister. By that time she had met more people in town, and while we remained friends we rarely saw each other again.

Decades have passed since the first time I saw Sahila, but we remain in touch; when she comes to Seattle for a medical conference we always get together for a cocktail or two and talk about our lives. There's a remarkable level of fluidity in our conversations that is hard to explain; we can pick up as though we saw each other every day, sharing a deep understanding of each others' struggles with identity. She was the first person I told that I had begun to identify as genderqueer, and she took it completely in stride, probably having recognized it in me long before others had. Surprising each other every time with the openness and depth of our conversations, we often talk about keeping touch in between those rare visits, but life always seems to get in the way.

Ghost

In retrospect, when I think through all the details of what drew me to her, and what helped us relate, I notice the telltale signs of my own gender identity that was so foreign to me then. I wonder, had I understood more about myself then, would I have been able to approach and relate to her differently? I will never know, but what I do know is that her ghost has always stayed with me, no longer an obsession, but forever a part of my journey. As a reminder, in the back of my medicine cabinet, behind a dozen dramatically sculpted flasks of designer cologne I've tried over the years, there is a small, non-descript bottle with a black plastic cap. The label is old and peeling, but still quite legible in the light: "THE BODY SHOP / *eau de toilette* / White Musk."

A Boy Named Su

Hubert

It was the first year of my graduate studies, and while I had stayed at the same institution, nearly all of my undergraduate friends had moved away. Two of the three roommates in my graduate dorm were former classmates, but while we liked and trusted each other well enough to live together, we had never been socially close. It felt like a reset – I could redefine myself however I wanted, and there was no one to call me out on my inconsistencies with my past self.

As an undergrad, there had been little to my life beyond studying. While I spent many a night pining after Sahila and the occasional Friday night dancing at Axis, most of my social time was working on assignments with my friends or going to dorm parties, and beyond a few short-lived misadventures I never dated. My parents and massive student loans were paying for my studies, and while I earned a little bit working as an undergraduate research assistant and at summer internships, I felt guilty spending time or money that wasn't directly related to my education. Now, though my graduate stipend was meager, it was enough to pay the bills, and for the first time in my life I was financially independent. It was a feeling of freedom that was entirely new to me.

Another part of myself I had suppressed during college was the joy of butt play. I was determined to make myself desirable to women, and I was trying to act as conventionally straight as possible to achieve that. While my classmates were orders of magnitude more accepting of homosexuality than my midwestern neighbors, and I had made a number of close gay friends, the binary of straight and gay was even more pronounced in college than it had been in high school. One had to be either straight or gay, with the possible exception of bisexuals, who were eyed with great skepticism from both sides. My strong attraction towards women coupled with a desire to be filled didn't fit into any of these labels. It was a time during which Freud had not yet fallen completely out of favor, and I thought that perhaps I had just gotten stuck in the "anal stage" and never progressed fully to the "genital stage" – it was time for me to just grow up and get over it.

With my newfound financial and social freedom, though, the feelings started coming back. In my solitary room, I fantasized about being touched and penetrated, but had no real outlet for these desires. Furthermore, despite my best engineering efforts, there was nothing like the weight bench of my youth to even make a decent sex toy. It was around this time that one of my roommates and I discovered that there was a bug in our graduate dorm's phone system whereby one could call "976" numbers for free. These were generally "adult" lines for chatting and personals. One could find them in the notorious back pages of the local alternative newspaper, the Boston Phoenix, usually charging a dollar a minute or more to call. For a brief moment in time, for a few horny graduate students, they cost nothing at all.

I never even tried meeting women through this system – I always assumed my next girlfriend would come from a more conventional setting. For me, this opportunity was all about satisfying my secret desires. I began listening through the voice personals of men looking for men, and was disappointed to find that most of them were for dating or hookups – not at all what I was looking for. I skipped ad after ad with touch tones until suddenly I heard a deep, slow voice with a gravelly Boston accent from what sounded like an older man. "Hello, this is Joseph. (pause) I'm looking for young, athletic college boys who would like a massage. (pause) I'm very good with my hands. (pause) No reciprocation necessary." I listened to the message over and over again, surprised at how turned on I was. The thought of lying face down on a table with some strong hands caressing my body, finding their way to my bottom and stimulating me there, was overwhelmingly seductive. I didn't picture at all what this person might look like; I was completely focused on the sensations I would be feeling. Eventually I timidly left a message with my real name (which I immediately regretted) and my phone number. I described myself as slim and athletic; the former was more true than the latter, but a summer of swimming had given me more definition than I'd ever had before then.

Joseph called me back the same day, and without my asking he reassured me it was just a massage, and he just liked the feeling of muscular young bodies under his hands. I didn't get into specifics about what I wanted, but quickly arranged a time for us to meet during the upcoming weekend. Already nervous about the risks I was taking, I picked a daytime meeting as it felt somewhat safer. He said he could come pick me up and take me to his place, so I gave him my dorm's address (again immediately regretting it). I hung up the phone, my heart beating incredibly fast, and extremely turned on. I masturbated several times over the next few days just fantasizing about the upcoming session.

Saturday was a perfect New England fall day: sunny, cool, and crisp, and I waited outside as we had discussed. No sign of Joseph. I waited fifteen minutes, then twenty, and then suddenly I saw a tiny beat-up car pull up, and a large, unkempt-looking man with scraggly hair struggle to get out of it, huffing and puffing his way towards me and waving.

Hubert

"Hubert!" he cried, "Are you Hubert?" I realized with some relief that he had misheard my name over the phone. I also felt all the desire draining from me, for while I hadn't pictured what Joseph might look like, this didn't feel right at all. The abstract hands now had a body and face attached to them, and it was a body and face I did not want to be close to, let alone be intimate with. Where would he take me in that beat-up car? Was it safe? Was he safe? What was I doing?

"Yes," I said, trying to swallow my doubts, "are you Joseph?"

"Yes, sorry I'm so late, I was trying to call you but you weren't answering. Wow, you look just like you said in your message," he said, looking me up and down.

I shifted uncomfortably. "Oh, yeah, I didn't hear your call because I've been waiting down here," I said.

"So this is my sister's car," Joseph continued in a rambling rapid-fire, not at all like the calm, firm voice in his message. "Because my car broke down, you see, and I have to bring it right back to her, so I can't meet up today, I'm sorry, that's why I was trying to call."

"Oh OK," I said with a feeling of immense relief – fate had intervened and I was going to be able to back out easily.

"Should we reschedule for next week?" he asked hopefully.

At this point I was certain I wanted nothing to do with Joseph, and said, "Uh, I'll be traveling next week," which was mostly true, at least for part of the week.

"No problem, so maybe call me when you get back?" he pressed on.

"Sure..." I said hesitantly – perhaps a bit too hesitantly.

His eyes narrowed a bit. "Well, you have my number, so give me a call, I'd love to see you." With that, he huffed and puffed back to his car and drove off.

I felt an incredible sense of relief come over me and walked to my lab with a sense of lightness and joy. I had dodged a bullet: what was I thinking, a promising research career ahead of me and I might have ended up being murdered in some dirty hovel by some crazy guy just to satisfy a twisted curiosity? I had to get myself together and focus on "normal" dating. That was quite the close call, quite the close call indeed, I told myself.

All of that revisionism fell apart by the time I reached my lab. I had gotten so close to satisfying my desires and then let it completely evaporate. I knew I wouldn't call Joseph back, and while in principle I could go back to the dating lines to find others, I never contacted anyone else. I took the experience as a sign that this was something too risky to explore, at least in terms of involving others, and I tried my best to bury those desires again.

As much as I tried, though, they would never remain below the surface for long. For many months afterwards, I would go back to the fantasy where I was face down on a comfortable massage table in a darkened room, and firm, dominant hands were caressing my body, my feet, my legs, and slowly parting my thighs to reach my bottom. I never imagined much detail about the person behind those hands, but I could only conceive of it being a male presence, as that was the nature of the binary. Only men could be dominant, only men would touch other men in that way, only gay (or bi) men would be interested in touching or being touched in that way.

How little I knew.

A Boy Named Su

Purim

After years of living in tiny undergraduate dorms, slightly less tiny graduate dorms, a decent but inconveniently located apartment with horrific flatmates, and a horrific but inconveniently located apartment with a decent flatmate, I had finally moved into an apartment I actually liked with someone reasonable. The early 20th-century brick building was in the heart of Cambridge, close to the T (subway) as well as Harvard Square. Our unit was a small but charming corner two-bedroom that overlooked the classical architecture of the square, and when the sun set through the sixth-floor bay windows, the brick facades of the buildings would glow with a beautiful red warmth. The oak floors were old and badly needed refinishing, the tiny galley kitchen was an afterthought in the hallway between the bedrooms and the living room, and the bathroom was fifty years out of date, but the location made it all perfect.

The only reason it was affordable was because our school owned the building – spots were highly coveted and opened up very rarely. I managed to get in through two friends, Mark and Amos, with whom I had become close over the previous year. A close friend of theirs was moving out of the building, and through a complicated arrangement of roommate and apartment-swapping, we were able to get our place.

Mark and Amos were also graduate students at my school, but seemed to be more interested in their next party than their next publication. They had devoted themselves to always knowing where the party was, and indeed, they always did. They styled themselves after the questionable protagonists in the 90s indie film *Swingers*, forever jumping from party to party chasing after "digits" (women's phone numbers). While their juvenile antics turned off nearly all of my other friends and grated on my own nerves at times, I was desperate to finally be popular and part of an active social scene. Most Friday and Saturday nights, Mark and Amos knew of multiple parties to choose from, and we did our best to get to all of them. Most were thrown by other graduate students, but their circle was impressively large – artists, filmmakers, musicians, journalists, and young office workers were all part of the scene.

I was also about halfway through my doctoral program at this point and past all of my requirements, so I had a lot more free time for social endeavors. I began spending most weekends with Amos and Mark, with my new roommate often tagging along. Amos and Mark were Jewish and in addition to the party scene were active in their community, and to bring me along they gifted me a yarmulke and introduced me as one of the Bene Israel (a small community of Jewish people in India) at Seder dinners and other social functions. I met some lovely young women through these events, though I never followed up to avoid the awkward conversation about not actually being Jewish.

Usually the brothers went to other people's parties rather than throwing their own, but Purim was an exception, and their party was known far and wide to be one of the best in our circle. The wearing of costumes is traditional for the celebration of Purim, but the brothers took it one step further and held "Boston's Only Purim Drag Party," as their emails loudly proclaimed. They went all out – they rented a small event space near Central Square, got a DJ, and set up professional lighting. I was a little apprehensive about the event as I'd never dressed in drag before, but these were my closest friends at the time and I wasn't going to miss their biggest party of the year. I helped them with the planning, and while I wasn't able to help with setup, I promised to stay late to help clean up.

In the weeks leading up to the event, I was obsessed with what I would wear and how I could put together a reasonable outfit on my tight graduate student budget. Amos, Mark, and I planned a trip to The Garment District, our local alternative used clothing store. Amos was small and wiry and settled on a loudly patterned housedress and a blond wig; Mark was tall and broad and picked a puffy prom dress that his copious chest hair burst through in all directions. They both ducked into the facility's not-so-private dressing rooms to try out their finds, coming out to laugh at themselves and each other a bit louder than was necessary. From their choices, comments, and laughter, it was clear they wanted to intentionally look as ridiculous as possible.

Though it would have been easy to play along and find a ridiculous outfit for myself, I knew this was not what I wanted. I quietly looked through the racks until I found a black spaghetti-strapped floor-length black cotton/spandex dress with a lacy pattern through the bodice that turned into a solid fitted skirt at the midriff. I was fairly certain it would fit me, and with a few modifications I thought it could be perfect. I didn't show it to my friends or try it on; I just grabbed a long wavy black wig and caught up with them at the cashier.

"What did you get?" they asked.

"Oh, you'll see at the party," I responded with a smile.

As soon as I got home, I locked my bedroom door, took off all my clothes, and slipped the dress over my naked body and a padded bra from the drugstore across the street. There was a momentary rush that took me by surprise – the feeling of that soft fabric clinging tightly to my skin, the air touching my bare shoulders and neck, and the swirl of the fabric at my hips, which all felt wonderful in a way I had not anticipated. I walked over to the mirror, elated, but all the wind instantly emptied from my sails. Instead of the beautiful transformation I experienced in my mind, I saw a skinny guy in a dress looking ridiculous, an awkward lump appearing where a sleek *mons pubis* should be. Still, I resolved to make the best of it. I cut the skirt part of the dress mid-thigh, put on the wig, and put on a black bra and some black lipstick I'd picked up at the drugstore. It was far from perfect, but it would be good enough.

Given how high I had cut the skirt, even my tiniest underwear was showing through, and not wanting to spend even more money on this failed costume I decided to just make something out of what I had. I took a pair of spandex bike shorts and cut out the front and back material to form a makeshift thong. I put it on, which again felt surprisingly wonderful, and put the dress back on. The lump was smoothed away, my underwear was no longer visible, and the short hem of the skirt and material brushing against my nearly-bare bottom felt exciting. I still didn't look the way I had imagined I would in those first moments in the dress, but at the least it felt like a good costume, and it felt good to wear it.

A Boy Named Su

The night of the party I was nervous both about how I would get to the location in my costume and how my outfit would look to others – at the time Boston was a fairly homophobic place and it was not at all unusual to hear of LGBTQ people getting jumped (or worse) in the street. I decided to take off the wig and wear a floor length coat so no aspect of the costume would be visible other than the black lipstick, which was popular enough with goth folks that it wouldn't raise many eyebrows. I walked into the party just as it was getting started, greeted Mark and Amos, went straight to the bathroom to put on my wig and fix my look, then walked out into the room and took off my coat. I took a deep breath and walked into the party.

Immediately I regretted my choice in outfit as I saw that every other guy at the party had gone for the same aesthetic as Mark and Amos – they had all picked outfits to specifically call out how ridiculous it was for them to wear a dress. Biceps bulged out of puffy sleeves, chest hair and beards were popping out everywhere, and big booming male voices and movements made it clear they were making no attempt at femininity; in fact they seemed to be making every effort to appear even more masculine than usual. I was beginning to feel a bit of panic when a tiny blonde woman suddenly caught me by the shoulders and looked me straight in my face.

"Su! You look AMAZING!" she cried.

It was Liv, Amos's on-again, off-again girlfriend. Liv was vocally bisexual, never followed any gender rules, and had taken an immediate liking to me the first time we met; I had more than a little bit of a crush on her. While she usually dressed across the gender spectrum, today she very intentionally wore the most feminine outfit she had; she would no more play by drag-party rules than by any others society attempted to place on her.

"Do you... do you really think so?" I asked skeptically.

I think she could tell how nervous I was, and I can't remember the exact details of what she said, but I remember her talking about the various parts of my outfit, which got me talking about how I had modified it, and she was really excited to hear about it all and the effort I had put into making it. I told her I still didn't look the way I had imagined I would.

"Well I think you look *beautiful*," she said with a smile, which made my heart glow with unexpected joy; I felt my anxiety begin to melt away in that warmth. She had *seen* me, including the femininity in me, and she had actually *liked* it! I smiled from ear to ear and thanked her, finally feeling good enough about myself to walk into the party. Pouring myself a drink, I stepped into the crowd to talk with my friends and meet some new people, dance, drink, and have a reasonably good time.

As promised, I stayed late that night to help Amos and Mark clean up. Near the end, Amos came up to me laughing, and said, "You won't believe this, but like five of my guy friends have come over to me and asked me to introduce them to that 'hot Indian chick you were talking to.'"

"Really?" I said, more thrilled than amused – I had no interest in meeting these men, but the fact that someone, anyone, had seen my femininity shine through despite the imperfection of my costume was still deeply exciting in a way I couldn't quite understand.

"I could introduce you if you'd like, ha ha ha," he continued, and I laughed along with his joke, not wanting to get into what I was really feeling inside. This put me in high spirits; maybe people could see my femininity more easily than I thought. What did that mean? What would I do with this knowledge? I was deep in my thoughts about this when I leaned over a table to pick up a wayward cup from a spilled drink.

"Woah, woah, Su, no, no, NO, nobody wants to see that!" I heard Amos and Mark yelling out with alarm and laughter. Amos and Mark were apparently both directly behind me, and I realize my short skirt must have risen, exposing my thong and hairless bottom. Suddenly the feeling of elation was completely gone, and I was filled with a deep sense of shame. What was I thinking? I wasn't feminine and sexy, I was disgusting and perverted, and I wanted to sink through the floor. *Nobody wants to see that.* The words would echo through my head for many years to come. Losing all the glow of my lifted spirits, I once again regretted every decision that had led to this outfit.

"Oh, yeah, ha ha, I guess I should put my coat on," I said awkwardly.

Amos just laughed, "Yeah, clean yourself up – just go home, we've got this taken care of."

"Uh, OK," I said, even more embarrassed, but thankful for a chance to escape.

"Go clean yourself up," they repeated, laughing, not intending to be hurtful, completely unaware of how deeply every word stung my fragile sense of self in that moment. I walked home quickly in my coat with my wig in my pocket, straining to avoid the hot tears that were forming in my eyes. I got inside, stripped off the dress and put it deep in my closet, washed the makeup off my face, and went straight to bed, wanting to forget the details of this night. I would never go out or even dress in drag in Cambridge again, and it was almost another decade before I went to another drag party.

How bright those first moments of public femininity were, but they were nothing in the face of a lifetime of stereotypes and shame. Still, those small sparks had felt their first breath of oxygen, and like the other desires I had never been able to "grow out of," they would eventually seek out and find new sources of fuel. For now, though, the embers would sleep deep beneath the surface, glowing dully in the darkness.

Babe in Toyland

I was halfway through my doctoral program, in the spring of my third year, reaching the end of one line of research and about to embark on another. Some colleagues at a corporate research lab on the west coast had reached out to see if I might want to join them for an internship, and while my advisor wasn't willing to let me go for the entire summer, we settled on a two-week research consultancy. The lab was in the suburbs of a major city with little in the way of public transportation or local restaurants, so the company set me up with a car and an efficiency suite in a modest hotel. While I had felt a first rush of freedom three years before when I became a graduate student, this was a whole new level – it was like a make-believe future life working at a company with my own apartment.

I spent ten to twelve-hour days at the lab, completely engrossed in the research I was working on with my new collaborators, mindful of the short timeline I had in which to demonstrate results. By 6pm, though, the lab would be mostly empty as the researchers went home to their families. For the nights, I was on my own, and on the very first day I arrived, I began to formulate a plan.

After stopping by a grocery store to pick up some pasta and vegetables to make a basic dinner in my tiny suite, I cracked open the room's heavy volume of yellow pages. I looked up "Adult Stores" and found a few in neighborhoods far enough away from my location and other stores that it would be very unlikely to see anyone from the lab. All of the stores had videos, of course, but I kept looking until I found what I was looking for – an ad that said "MAGAZINES – VIDEOS – BOOTHS – *TOYS*." Oh yes: toys.

My heart was already racing and I was too nervous to go that first night, but the very next evening I went straight from work, not giving myself the chance to lose my nerve again. As I drove over, I thought about what I was hoping to find there. I had not had anything inside me since the days of the long smooth shaft of my home weight bench; though I'd had the privacy of my own room for years now, I had convinced myself that I needed to grow out of that desire. As time had gone on, though, I missed it more and more, and now I had an opportunity to move beyond homemade stimulators and buy toys actually meant for this purpose, without any risk of running into friends on the street like I would have back in Cambridge.

If the shaft from a weight bench could have felt that wonderful, I could hardly imagine how a toy specifically designed for anal pleasure might feel.

While I was generally thorough about my research on most things professional and personal, I didn't have internet at the hotel and knew better than to search for butt toys at my work computer. My only option was to wing it. I drove into the store's parking lot and turned off the engine, wondering whether I would actually have the nerve to walk in. For a good fifteen minutes I pretended to have just stopped there to peer studiously at a map, taking deep breaths as I tried to calm myself. Few people were going in and out of the store, and the only other store nearby was a restaurant that seemed to be closed, so to my relief, the odds of a chance encounter were extremely low.

Finally building up my nerve, I walked quickly into the store, past the clerk who never looked up, past a large front area full of magazines, past an even larger area with videos and booths, and finally to a few racks of toys in bright, garish packaging. I didn't know anything about types of materials, shapes, or brands at that time, so I just tried to make the best guesses I could. Most of the toys were of the "adult novelty" variety, made of cheap shiny rubber and visible through plastic clamshell cases, but it hardly mattered to me. I was completely fascinated by the varieties in shape and size – there were toys with ripples, bumps, curls, and bends; toys that were long, short, thick, and thin; toys that were blue, green, translucent, and silver; you name it, they had it. In the smaller men's section, there were toys crafted to look like erect penises (which I studiously avoided, still afraid of what that would imply), but most were more traditional butt plugs – they had a bulbous shape that grew smoothly from a narrow tip to the widest point, then tapered rapidly to a finger-like width (presumably for the sphincter to close on) and then flared out again to form a base. From my painful childhood superball experience I knew how forcefully my sphincter could try pull an object into my body, and immediately appreciated the thoughtful design of the base.

I decided to go with the traditional bulb shape, but that still left the question of size. Some were obviously too large to fit in my tiny body, and some were so small I knew I would hardly feel them. I picked a shiny black one on the larger side of what I thought I could handle, perhaps an inch and a half in diameter at its widest point. As it had been a while since I had played with my bottom, I also picked a second "starter" plug that was far smaller, with a relatively narrow profile about the size and shape of my middle finger, cast in a lovely translucent blue.

I could hardly breathe as I brought the items to the counter, looking away from any other customers I saw along the way (I remember being surprised to see an attractive woman in a business suit in the video aisle), but the cashier was too bored to even look at me while I bought the items. In later years, buying high-quality silicone sex toys from sex-positive stores, every purchase would come with an engaging discussion about safety tips, appropriate lubes, and cleaning strategies, along with a celebratory bow on a bright sex-positive bag. My first sex toy purchase would have no such fanfare – the cashier unceremoniously dropped the packages into a brown paper sack and handed me my receipt (I remember wondering why – did anybody ever return sex toys? Or better yet, file them as business expenses?).

Giddy with excitement, I got in my rental car and stopped at the grocery store to pick up some K-Y Jelly before heading back to my room. I peeled off my clothes, arranged myself on the bed, and started by just putting the K-Y on my bottom. I hadn't put anything but Vaseline there before then, and the cool, smooth lube was a far silkier and more liquid feeling than I'd experienced before – just massaging the outside and letting the tip of my finger slip inside felt so wonderful, not to mention the anticipation of what was coming next. I coated the body of the smaller blue plug with lube and slowly slid it in all the way to the base, closing my sphincter around its narrow shaft, and closing my eyes with pleasure. It felt so wonderful, and despite all the shame I had felt in the intervening years I immediately realized what a fool I had been to deny myself this sensation. Besides, if I could pleasure myself in this way on my own, where nobody else could see, what harm could there possibly be?

After spending a few minutes with the smaller plug, I was even more excited to try the larger one. If the small one felt that good, surely the large one would feel amazing. I opened the package, lubed it up, and started to push it in, quickly realizing I had grossly overestimated how large a plug I could handle. I could only get the first part of the tip inside, and while that felt nice, I really wanted to feel the whole thing inside me. I pushed as best I could from an awkward angle and could feel myself opening up a little farther and getting a little more in, but I couldn't get anywhere near largest part of the plug. I was extremely turned on but also extremely frustrated, and decided to end the night by re-inserting the blue plug and masturbating.

This was the first time I had masturbated with something inside me – when I was playing the weight bench shaft in my youth I had not yet learned how to cum, and once I had learned I never tried combining the two, as I was too distracted by the new pleasures of touching myself in my room. Now, as I started touching myself with the blue plug inside me, I could feel something was different, more intense, with my sphincter opening and closing around the thin shaft. When I came, feeling my back arch and my whole body grip the shaft tightly, I realized there was an entire dimension to the experience I had been missing out on.

The next night I tried the big plug again, determined to get it inside me. I decided I needed more leverage than pushing on it with my hands, so I set it up on the seat of a tightly stuffed arm chair, kneeled down on the seat on top of the plug, and slowly lowered my body onto it. I was immediately getting much farther than I had before, sliding up and down, pushing a little harder each time, and on that first night of this I quickly reached a point where I pushed too hard. I felt a sharp pain shoot through me, pulled myself off the armchair and walked in rapid circles, trying to clear the sensation. Thankfully the pain was momentary, but my arousal was completely gone; I wasn't even interested in masturbating at that point, and gave up for the night.

This was to be my life for the next two weeks – every day going to the lab to make new scientific discoveries with my colleagues, then every night coming home to make new sexual discoveries with my body. Many nights ended in pain and sometimes even a little bleeding, but most just ended in frustration and a masturbation session with the blue plug. I was learning my limits: how much lube I needed, how much I had to warm myself up, how slowly I needed to coax myself further and further open – still I could still never make it all the way around the large plug's substantial girth.

Just a few days before I was to go back to Boston, after a week and a half of increasingly aggressive practice, something changed. I felt a bit of pain but not enough to stop, and I could feel with my fingers that I was at the very edge of getting the plug all the way in. I added more lube and tried to relax my entire body as best I could, and suddenly, with a sharp, shooting pain, it was inside me. The first few moments were like every other time I had gone too far – the pain was all I could focus on and I instantly lost my erection. Then, as I realized the plug was finally inside me, and my sphincter could close around the entire plug, pulling it even further inside, I felt a fullness unlike any I had felt before. Suddenly I understood the purpose of the sharp angle before the flared base – it not only allowed that ridge to provide a powerful stimulation to the area just inside the rectum, but a small amount of squeezing would cause the plug to move considerably inside my body, which felt absolutely heavenly.

My erection came back with a vengeance, and I spent the next few glorious minutes squeezing and releasing the plug inside my body. Eventually I couldn't keep my hands off myself and began to masturbate. While touching myself with the blue plug inside had felt great, this was a whole new experience. The absolute fullness and motion as I squeezed it in and out was incredible, and when I finally came, squeezing down hard on the plug, I had the kind of eye-closing, body-shuddering orgasm I hadn't felt since my first time on the yellow bean bag.

I was worried that taking the plug out would be as painful as it had been going in, but in fact it was no problem at all. I noticed a small amount of bleeding, but had seen that on previous nights and wasn't concerned; I went to sleep very satisfied that night.

On the few nights I had left in my private room, I was never able to get it all the way in again, which made me even more frustrated than before. By this time, I also had less time to myself, as my research colleagues wanted to take me out for final dinners and drinks on the last few evenings. I had planned to throw the toys out, bringing no evidence of this experience back to Boston, but after all the trouble I had gone through to procure them and all the pleasure they had helped me achieve, I knew there was no way I was going to leave them behind. I wrapped them in my clothes and hoped with all my heart that the security agents at the airport wouldn't find them or ask awkward questions. Fortunately, nothing of the sort happened, and I was able to unpack and hide them away back in my room in Cambridge.

The toys immediately became a regular part of my masturbatory routine at home. I was only able to get the full large plug inside me one more time, and that time resulted in considerably more pain. After that, I noticed that the plug was constructed as a shiny rubber layer on top of a flexible core, and cut away the outer layer to reveal the slightly smaller plug.

This was far easier to get inside me, and while it didn't give me quite the feeling of the original plug, it was so much easier and less painful, it became my toy of choice when I wanted to feel filled up inside.

In my mind, just as it had been in my youth, I compartmentalized this kind of play as a secret mode of pleasure I would only explore on my own. I would have my "normal", cis-het dating relationships with women, and then in the privacy of my room I would have a special technique for intense pleasure known only to me. I no longer fooled myself into thinking I would grow out of it, but I was certain I would never speak of it to others. Surely no woman would accept such a shameful thing.

Or so I thought.

"The Best Boyfriend in the World"

"Well, do you have a pen?" she asked. It was the first time I had ever worked up the nerve to ask a woman for her phone number; I had waited until she was about to leave, and now I was kicking myself for not having thought through this most obvious of details. In future years, at least until pulling out a smartphone became socially acceptable, I would always carry two pens, in case I lent one out or it ran out of ink. Tonight all I had was a rapidly growing feeling of panic. Seeing the anxiety in my face, she broke the tension with a laugh, "Don't worry, I've got one." She tore off the corner of an envelope from her purse and wrote "KATE" in capital letters along with her phone number. She handed it to me, giggled, and yelled out, "Call me!" over her shoulder as she walked out of the room.

I had gone to the party with Amos and Mark, and after congratulating me for "getting digits," they got into a fierce debate with each other over how many days I should wait before calling her. I mostly ignored their ranting, knowing for me the real challenge would be working up the nerve to call her at all. I pinned the torn piece of envelope to my office wall, and after staring at it for a good three days, I gave her a call the following Tuesday.

She was happy to hear from me, as friendly and fun on the phone as I remembered her being from the party; we chatted for half an hour before I asked her if she wanted to go out on a date. She readily agreed and asked when we should meet, and I replied that I was about to leave to visit another lab for the next two weeks (see "Babe in Toyland") and we could work out the details before I came back, buying myself some time to think of what we would actually do. She agreed, and we said goodbye.

I was ecstatic. Kate was a recent pre-med graduate who was working in Boston for a year to save up before starting medical school; she had a sharp wit coupled with a warm smile and ready laugh, and as a distance runner had the slim, athletic build that I have always been most attracted to. In many ways, she was what I had imagined to be the perfect girlfriend, and I had unrealistic expectations about how well this would all work out. Fortunately the research consultancy distracted me from obsessing about her too much; I called her from that office once to work out the details of our date, but otherwise she was just on the periphery of my mind, part of the life I would return to when the consultancy ended.

I flew back to Boston with growing anxiety about the date and only a few days to prepare myself. We decided to meet at a small bar just on the Boston side of the Harvard Bridge, and despite the nervous afternoon I'd spent in anticipation, it went surprisingly well. I was immediately comfortable with her and she with me, and before we parted ways that night we had already planned out a second date. Soon there was a third and a fourth, and by the time a month had passed we were seeing each other at least twice a week, usually going to her place and making dinner together. She and her roommate were both trying to save money for med school, so they had rented a small one-bedroom near their jobs at Boston College. Kate's roommate had the bedroom and paid a little extra, while Kate had most of the small living room, cordoned off with an imperfect system of drapes. That curtained refuge is where we would spend much of our time together.

While Koko and I had been physical with each other, we had been so new to the territory that it was more about discovery rather than intimacy; we never even spent the night together. With Kate there was an immediate emotional connection to our touch, and for the first time since childhood I felt the warm glow of physical closeness building an intimate bond between us. It didn't hurt that we were incredibly attracted to each other as well. All the concerns I'd had about my sexuality and attractiveness faded into the background, and I reveled in the mutual feeling of desire. The first time she asked me to spend the night with her I immediately agreed, and felt for the first time the warm joy of holding someone close through the night and waking up with them in the morning. At twenty-two and twenty-four, Kate and I were both still virgins, and despite our hunger for each other, we would keep our underwear on and do everything we could with our hands and bodies despite that barrier. That was how we intended to keep things, as well – or so I thought.

As the weeks went on, Kate started arranging moments of greater privacy for us that I was completely oblivious to. At first it was nights when her roommate was staying at her boyfriend's place so that we'd have the place to ourselves. Next it was a trip to Woods Hole to see her former research lab, a couple of hours out of town. We borrowed her roommate's car, and after spending a lovely New England fall day walking hand in hand through the tiny village, as the sun began to set she asked if I wanted to get a room at a local inn and just go home the next day.

"Why?" I asked, "it's only a couple of hours to get back home." Despite finally being financially independent, I was only scraping by on my graduate stipend, and was extremely cost-conscious at that time. This was the only lens through which I could think about her question, and staying at an inn seemed like an unnecessary and extravagant expense.

"Fine, I just thought it might be fun," she said, laughing it off. She was a little quiet on the way home, but I hardly noticed.

A couple of weeks later she asked what I was doing that weekend, and I mentioned a few parties Amos and Mark had lined up.

"But I have plans for us!" she protested.

She wanted to take a road trip Mount Washington, the windiest spot in New England; her roommate and her boyfriend would come along as a double date so we'd be able to use their car. She had planned out the route and everything we'd need.

"We could even get a hotel out there," she said tentatively.

I was already running the numbers through my head. "Well, that would be pretty expensive, why don't we just leave earlier so we can get back."

"I just thought it would be romantic," she said, clearly disappointed, which I did notice, but knowing she wanted to save money as well I felt I was making the best decision for both of us.

The Friday night before we were to leave, she called me to tell me her roommate and her boyfriend had fallen sick and had to drop out. Rather than take the opportunity to spend some time alone with Kate on a romantic trip, I'm embarrassed to say my first thought was again the cost.

"Well, that will mean we'll have to rent a car, so the cost will double for each of us," I said. Racking my brain for a solution, I continued, "Hmm, let me see if my friend Markus wants to join."

"Um, ok..." she said hesitantly.

Markus was my best friend, a Swedish graduate student who was visiting our lab for a year, and while she didn't have anything against Markus *per se*, she was often annoyed as she felt I spent more time with him than her. This was in fact the case: we worked together all day in the same lab and often hung out in the evening since we lived across the street from each other. I chalked up her hesitation to this, and went off to check with Markus, who enthusiastically agreed. Years later, Markus would tell me he knew what a stupid move this was on my part, but really wanted to see Mount Washington and figured if I didn't realize what a fool I was being that it was mostly my fault. In retrospect, it's hard to blame him.

The trip was a lot of fun – Mount Washington was as windy as promised, and the beautiful New England fall colors made even the long drive there quite spectacular. Before we left the mountain she asked again, hesitantly this time, if maybe we should get a couple of rooms at an inn. She saw me pause and didn't even wait for my answer.

"Oh, nevermind" she said quickly and turned away.

Kate was quiet for most of the drive home; I noticed but was clueless about why. Markus, though, talked up a storm, perhaps to break the awkwardness between Kate and myself. We dropped him off at his apartment and then headed for her place. I made a few attempts at conversation which she quickly shut down.

Just as we finally found a parking spot, she said "You know, I think I'd rather be alone tonight if that's OK."

I was taken off guard. "Oh, uh, OK – is everything all right?"

"Yeah, it's fine," she said quickly, "I'd just rather be alone."

"Okay," I replied, kissed her goodbye, and headed for the T stop, still oblivious to what was going on.

In a few days she was back to the giggly warmth I had grown to love, and we happily planned our next night together, another evening where her roommate was going to be away. We made pasta with homemade sauce together, laughing and flirting with each other as in the best of times. We drank a couple more glasses of cheap wine than usual, put away the dishes, and crawled into bed together. Our attraction for each other had only grown over time, and that night we were touching each other more boldly than we ever had. At one point I was nuzzling the inside of her thighs, pushing aside her panties just enough to touch and kiss the soft skin on the borders of her vulva. She was pushing my head into her body, and in a quiet voice with ragged breath I had never heard from her, she asked, "Su, do you want to have sex?"

For a moment everything in my mind stopped, and I froze. This is a question I had been waiting to hear my entire adult life. As a child I had grown up hearing the sounds of my father trying to have sex with my mother and my mother fighting him off night after night. I had become convinced that only men wanted sex and that women never did, but women tolerated it for the sake of pleasing men. Furthermore, I was certain that if a woman ever did ask for sex, it was only because she knew this was what the man wanted, and the best possible answer a man could give would be "no." For her, this would be a welcome departure from the typical sex-crazed man who would demand sex in order to stay in the relationship.

As a consequence, despite every fiber of my body wanting to shout "YES," I thought my way through this convoluted logic and said after a brief pause, "No, I think we should wait."

"Okay," she said in a small voice and then was silent.

I, on the other hand, was patting myself on the back. "I really am the best boyfriend in the world," I thought to myself,

"What other guy would suppress his own desires to give her the answer she *really* wants?"

Within minutes, she mentioned it was getting late and asked if we could just go to sleep, and I happily curled up with her, extremely proud of my noble behavior.

The next morning was uneventful when I left for work, but after trying to call her for the next few days I was surprised that she never called back; typically she would never screen my calls if she were home and almost always called me back the same day. By Friday night I was getting genuinely worried about her when I got the call.

"Su?" she asked tentatively.

"Kate!" I said, relieved, "I've been trying to reach you all week, are you okay?"

"Su," she said, again, "I don't think you really want to be with me," she said, tears in her voice.

"What are you talking about?" I said, incredulous, "is this about Markus coming on that trip to Mount Washington?"

"What? No! You know what I'm talking about," she said.

"I don't," I pleaded, growing more desperate in my confusion.

"Are you even attracted to me?" she cried.

"Of course, Kate, why would you say that?" I asked.

"*You know*," she said, with angry tears.

"Are you breaking up with me?" I asked, still shocked, now expecting the worst.

"Well that's what you want, isn't it?" she responded.

"No, Kate, I..." I paused briefly, not sure how to continue.

"Goodbye, Su," she said, hanging up.

I was completely stunned. I genuinely had no idea what had happened, and it would be years before I understood. I told Markus about the phone call, as well as my close friends and officemates Brad and Mahnoor. They consoled me but could offer no explanations. I hadn't told them the details of that fateful night, since in my mind that was one of my best moments in the relationship and didn't even enter my mind as a possible cause. I was trying to figure out what I might have done or said before or after that point that led to the breakup. Eventually, I decided it must have been my cost-consciousness, something I was aware of and already a little embarrassed about.

Years later an unexpected conversation in a book club discussion of *The English Patient* led me to a stunning realization. A woman in my book club was articulating how Hana and Kip's unrequited physical relationship frustrated her emotionally and physically, reminding her of some of her own experiences

– experiences which were uncannily similar to what I had subjected Kate to. Hearing it firsthand, from a woman who was clearly not motivated by pleasing a man (our book club had very limited flirting potential), and speaking so frankly about desire, finally forced me to see the truth. Women *did* want to have sex; they had sexual appetites just as men did.

To me this was revolutionary; it went against everything I had ever believed about sexuality and gender – just like all the other binaries I had believed in, I had been certain men pursued women for sex and *never* the other way around. I had seen media representations of the opposite, but I had chalked it up to Hollywood catering to male fantasies as opposed to reflecting any kind of reality. The truth, of course, was that there was a far more simple explanation.

After a sleepless night, I remember running into my office at work the next morning and almost yelling to Brad and Mahnoor, "I just figured it out!"

"Figured out what?" Brad asked, pulling off his headphones.

"Why Kate broke up with me!" I said, my face flushed.

"Okay, why?" Brad continued.

"She broke up with me because I wouldn't have sex with her!!" I said triumphantly, as if I had just solved a major mystery (in my mind, I had).

"And?" they both asked.

I was stunned again. "Wait, you knew?"

"Well, sure," Mahnoor said, "once you told us you were sleeping with her but weren't having sex with her, we figured it was only a matter of time before you either had sex or she would give up on you."

"But you don't know the whole story," I said, almost in tears, and told them what had happened that fateful night. "She actually *did* want to have sex with me," I said.

"Oh, Su," Mahnoor said, in a sad and caring voice, "Why would you ever think she *didn't*?"

I realized two things at that moment. First, it was now certain that I had been completely wrong in my impressions of sex. Second, I felt that there was something deeply broken inside of me, that my entire mental programming about sex was clearly wrong, and now the prospect of entering into a sexual relationship seemed like an insurmountable barrier. I didn't identify with the forceful sexuality that I associated with my father, nor could I identify with the braggadocio of my male friends like Mark and Amos, and I had been so afraid that I'd be forcing myself on Kate that I wouldn't even have sex with her when she explicitly asked me to. How was I ever going to be masculine in a way that would work for me, but still be able to have sex with the women who wanted that from me?

"The Best Boyfriend in the World"

I wondered whether at twenty-four I was destined to be a virgin forever; I already felt too old given my friends' extensive experiences at that age. At the same time, I felt too young to become a hermit, but who would possibly have the patience to undo all those years of misconceptions, and how would I ever get past the shame of even admitting my broken state to them?

It would be so much safer to not even try.

A Boy Named Su

Kitty Phone Sex

After Kate there was a long desert of intimacy, made only more palpable by having experienced that level of warmth and closeness for the first time. I asked for a few phone numbers at parties and went on a few dates, but the anxiety that had started to grow in me around sex and intimacy after Kate was only becoming worse with time. In fact, the more I thought about it, the worse it became, and I avoided any connection that looked like it was heading in that direction. I did start dating one woman more regularly during that time, Tiffany, who I met unexpectedly when testing out a new personals service.

Tiffany was a young professional who felt out of my league in every dimension, from her perfect outfits to her stylish glasses to her acerbic wit. She could read me extremely well, which allowed to her to learn much more about me than I was willing to tell. One night when out at a bar she asked from out of the blue, "So what kinds of sex do you like?" Completely taken aback I started to stammer out some kind of reply, and her eyes grew wide.

"Wait a minute, you're a *virgin* aren't you?" emphasizing the word with a smile. Without waiting for me to answer, she said "You are, you ARE!" I didn't deny it, and her smile grew even larger. "We're going to have to fix that, aren't we?" What should have been a joyful moment for this young virgin, though, was one of abject terror.

From that point on, all she wanted to talk about was planning when and how we would have sex. She talked about the movie we should watch beforehand, what we should eat, what she would wear, whether we should keep the lights on or off. To this day I'm not sure if she was more obsessed with me or my virginity. At a party at my apartment during that period, while taking a photo together, I put my hand on her waist. "Lower," she said, and I moved my hand slightly lower. "LOWER," she said, more emphatically, and I again moved my hand slightly lower on her waist. With an exasperated sigh she grabbed my hand and put it squarely on her bottom. My instinct was to pull it away, but she firmly held my hand in place with hers.

Over time, I was growing more and more terrified of her. For a few weeks I would make excuses at our dates about having to get home early, and at some point when she cornered me on the phone about why I was avoiding her, instead of talking to her I just stopped answering her calls altogether. She kept trying to reach me for a week or so before giving up; I never contacted her or heard from her again. I felt a sense of relief for not having to deal with my anxiety around sex, but also immense frustration at having pushed away an open invitation from someone I was extremely attracted to. I had managed to make myself both more miserable and more frustrated than I had been before, with little outlet for either feeling.

In the midst of that emotional storm, I turned to the racy ads in the back pages of the Boston Phoenix. I had always wondered about phone sex and chat lines since the time I'd tried the 976 numbers (see "Hubert"), and I managed to find a chatline that was only ten cents per minute for men (and free for women), much cheaper than the others since all the men and women were individual callers and not paid staff. The setup was simple: you recorded a name and a greeting, then released it into the system, which allowed you to listen to others' ads, send messages back and forth, and even chat live. Your ad remained on the system only for the duration of your call, so you could try a new approach every time.

Despite my frugality, I was desperate for contact, and I started calling regularly. I recorded my greetings and would go online with a different approach each night but would almost never match with any women. Interest from another caller was signified by a special tone, and I would be lucky if I heard it once per session. The few times I did match I had a hard time holding the woman's attention, and they would abruptly move on to the next caller while I was mid-sentence. I suspected that maybe I just didn't have the right kind of message or the right kind of voice, and I came up with a brilliant plan to find out what was wrong – I would call as a woman and see what other men's greetings were like so I could improve my own pitch.

The first time I called, I picked the name Kitty out of the blue, and just in case anyone I knew might recognize my voice, I disguised it with my interpretation of a British accent. I recorded my name, and what I thought was a very basic greeting – "Hello, this Kitty, and I'm just wondering if anyone out there wants to talk tonight," in my flirtiest, most feminine British accent. I listened to the playback, which sounded reasonably convincing, and pressed the tone to accept the message and release it into the system.

I heard one or two men's ads before the onslaught began. Not only did the tones start ringing for messages being sent to me, I was getting nonstop requests to chat live. So many requests were coming in that I could no longer hear men's ads, only their direct messages and requests to chat. Part of me was completely bewildered, but another part was strangely thrilled at this attention; I quickly forgot my original mission of learning what an effective greeting should sound like.

After listening to a few of these requests to chat I heard a deep, gruff voice that said, "All right, Kitty, I'm going to tell you exactly what to do. You just let me take care of you. Love to chat." Something inside me was responding to this firm, demanding voice, and I very much wanted to be taken care of. I accepted the chat and held my breath, my heart beating intensely in my chest.

"Hello?" the gruff voice called out.

"Hi, this is Kitty," I said demurely.

"Hi Kitty, this is David. I love your accent, where are you from?" he asked.

"Thank you, I'm from London."

"Oh, that's great," he said. "What are you doing right now, Kitty?"

"Oh, nothing much, just playing with myself," which was true – I had already stripped off my clothes and was tending to a painfully strong erection. "What would you *like me* to do?" I asked in as sultry a way as I could manage.

"What are you wearing right now?" he asked.

"I'm completely naked," I replied honestly.

"Oh, that's great," he said (he was not one much for words). "Kitty I want you start rubbing yourself, slowly, just back and forth," he said, his voice thickening.

"Mmmm, oh yeah...." I said, stroking my cock more and more rapidly, watching the clear drops of precum form at the tip, a sure sign that I was extremely turned on.

"Now I want you to just keep doing that, how does that feel?" he continued.

"Mmmmm it feels wonderful, mmmm," I said, and it did feel wonderful – I could tell I was getting close to the edge.

"Oh, your voice is so sexy Kitty," he grunted, his breath getting heavier and louder; I could tell he was masturbating now as well.

"Mmmmmm... MMMMMM," I managed to get out, before without warning, I came all over myself. I instantly felt a wave of shock and remorse and said a quick "goodbye" and hung up the phone. I was embarrassed and ashamed at what I'd done, but also extremely turned on, my body still heaving from the most intense orgasm I'd had in months. One thing was for certain: I was going to make that call again.

For the next few months, I called the line almost every night, always as Kitty, always naked. Some nights I would use my butt plugs, at first pretending they were dildos I was putting in my vagina, then as I became more daring talked about them as butt plugs, which seemed to turn my listeners on even more. The men I chose to talk to fit a profile – generally gruff, taciturn types. Their dialog was rarely very interesting; their attempts at creativity would often be off-putting – I remember one man, attempting to be sensual, suggested he would put a dildo on his drill and "literally drill my ass," which sounded both painful and ridiculous; I hung up immediately. Most were like David, just telling me to stimulate myself, relishing the sound of my voice and my moans as I did so. I was sometimes surprised at the range of sounds I would make while turned on; Kate and Koko had both complained that I was extremely quiet while we were being intimate. Somehow these scenarios unlocked something in me, a vocally submissive part of myself that loved being "taken care of."

The calls were never very long; either I or they would come before too many minutes had passed, at which point I would sink back into my feelings of shame about the experience. If I thought I was abnormal before, this was only making it worse, wasn't it? I tried to convince myself it was OK for a variety of reasons – I knew what men liked because I was a man; this was just a way to masturbate and just a fantasy, not something I would do in real life; and the most ridiculous reason of all – that it was cheaper than calling as a man.

Once or twice I would match up with a woman who was calling the line to meet other women, and this experience surprised me in a different way. While I usually felt a lot of anxiety around talking to new women and had a hard time keeping a conversation going, these women were incredibly easy to talk to. In those conversations, it wasn't the usual session of moaning and masturbation, but I would actually get to know them a little and enjoy our chat. Every time, though, when they started asking for more details and wanted to meet, I would quickly end the call, afraid of being found out.

This would have gone on for many more months were it not for the last call. It was late on the night of July 4th; I had come home from the fireworks and was expecting a quick session before going to bed. The person I matched with had the kind of voice I liked, but once we connected he started going into how he had just had a horrible night. Apparently he had been on a boat for the fireworks and his girlfriend had ended up making out with another guy, and he had been attracted to this other woman on the boat but didn't make a move because he still felt committed to his girlfriend. "It sucks, you know," he said.

My horniness had long since melted away, and now I felt unable to hang up like I usually would since this person was clearly suffering. I could tell how much he needed someone to talk to, and I stayed on the line with him for hours, helping him think through his relationship. I felt drained, but at least I was able to help a fellow human being in crisis.

At the very end, he started asking me what I was wearing, and whether I wanted to masturbate with him. I was not at all interested – while anonymous dominance had been thrilling and sexy, hearing someone who I'd helped for hours with his problem just objectify me into a masturbatory aid was just way too much. If anything, I expected a basic "thank you." I hung up in frustration and anger.

Over the years I called the line a few more times, but it never felt the same again. I was not yet ready to really explore the intense feelings of desire that had come up during some of the calls, and the last call had so inured me to the experience that I didn't want to go through it again. "At least all that is behind me," I half-convinced myself, but there was a part of me that was beginning to realize that these aspects of my sexuality and desire were not going to be so easily suppressed.

A Boy Named Su

A Friend of Jen's

It was a Saturday night late in the Boston summer. The city sweltered in the throes of a muggy New England heat wave, and Markus and I were out in search of a house party. It was just the two of us: in the past, Amos and Mark would have been with us, but since Kate and I had broken up, I had started to distance myself from them. I had realized that whatever my notion of masculinity was going to be, it wouldn't really match with theirs. Besides, by this time, I had met most of the people in their circles, found my own friends amongst them, and grown those relationships into a wide sphere of people and events in the greater Boston area. Still, on that particular night, there were no events that we were aware of.

In the void of the friendship with Amos and Mark, Markus had become an important part of my life, the first "best friend" I'd had since high school. He was visiting our lab for a year from his university in Sweden, and we hit it off instantly. He had a European fashion sense which fit my style better than most of my peers and an irreverent sense of humor and wordplay that made every conversation a joy. We started out having lunch and dinner together at the lab, and when he ended up finding an apartment across the street from me, our friendship was sealed. We'd spend ten or twelve hours in the lab seven days a week, then every weekend evening we'd head to one of our places to make food, have a couple of cocktails, and head out to the evening's parties.

Our drink of choice was a Tanqueray gin and tonic with fresh-squeezed limes; when we didn't feel like cooking we'd just put Blue Stilton on a French baguette and pair it with our cocktails. Markus was constantly annoyed at how Bostonians called anything sophisticated or fashion-forward "European," so we jokingly referred to this quick dinner as a "European meal." We figured we'd save money by having drinks and food at home, but it also gave us a chance to talk about everything under the sun and build our bond with each other. Before long, people started commenting on how we would always appear together and leave together at parties. While we were both ostensibly trying to meet women, our friends would jokingly refer to us as a couple. Given how misunderstood we both already were, he for his European sensibilities and me for my lack of standard masculinity, it neither surprised nor particularly bothered us.

A Friend of Jen's

One day, months before this particular night, when Amos and I were still hanging out regularly, we considered the hypothetical of not knowing about any parties for a given Saturday night. I asked him what one might do under those challenging circumstances.

Amos frowned and furrowed his brow. "There are so many parties in the area – how could there not be a party?" he asked incredulously.

"Well, maybe just not a party we know about," I replied.

"Hmm," Amos said. "Well, the best bet would probably be to head to Davis Square, which has the highest density of grad students, and then just start making ever-widening circles around there until you hear a party."

This sounded ridiculous to me, but I decided to play along. "OK, but what then? You can't just walk in to a party where you don't know anyone!" I said.

He tilted his head. "If you have a six pack or a bottle of wine, they'll let you in," he responded with confidence.

"OK..." I said, "But what if they ask who you know?" We were both laughing at this point, it all seemed so far-fetched.

"Easy - tell them you're a friend of Jen's!" he shouted.

"Why *Jen*?" I asked, still laughing.

"There's always someone named Jen," he said, and that was that.

I had told this story to Markus earlier on this party-less evening while we were still finishing our gin and tonics, and to my dismay, he wanted to give it a try.

"Let's go for it!" he said.

"We can't *actually* do that," I said, surprised he was taking it seriously.

"Why not?" he countered.

I didn't really have a good response, so we went and bought a couple of six packs of Heineken (a sufficiently "European" beer to be considered sophisticated) and were on our way to the T stop.

Davis Square was surprisingly quiet that night, and after ten to fifteen minutes of circling the station we were about ready to give up. Then, turning on to a side street, we heard the tell-tale sounds of a party conversation coming from an upstairs window. We walked up to the front door and found a stocky woman in a sleeveless t-shirt with short, dark hair having a cigarette as she scanned the street.

"Hi," I said in my friendliest voice, "We're here for the party?"

A Friend of Jen's

She looked us up and down with no small degree of skepticism. "Who do you know here?" she asked, her eyes narrowing.

"I'm a friend of Jen's!" I responded brightly, without skipping a beat.

Her eyes lit up with familiarity and warmth. "Oh, great! She's upstairs right now, she might be in the bathroom!"

"Great!" we both said, introducing ourselves to her, and then walking up the stairs, laughing to each other that it had actually worked.

When we reached the top of the stairs, we understood why she had been so skeptical. We were the only men at the party, and most of the women there were in obvious couples. Nobody really seemed to mind our presence, though, so we opened a couple of our beers, handed bottles around to others at the party, and started chatting. The women at the party were welcoming and kind, and we were more than happy to have salvaged the night and ended up at a fun party with lovely people; clearly we'd also have quite a story to tell.

One particular person, though, kept catching my eye - a beautiful, slender woman with gold ringlets and lovely wrinkles around her eyes that would appear every time she smiled, which was wonderfully often. I kept shyly looking at her when I thought she wasn't looking, though once or twice I saw her notice and she flashed a smile at me. Given my usual shyness, I would immediately look away.

I had just poured myself a cup of wine when she walked past me into a darkened room and beckoned at me with a finger and a smile. I put down my cup and followed her; she closed the door behind us. I was so thrilled she wanted to talk to me I gave her a hug, and she said with surprise, "Oh! Thank you for that!"

"Of course!" I returned, with no idea as to what was coming next.

"I'm Kay," she responded, smiling up at me.

"Hi Kay, I'm Su," I replied, both incredibly attracted to her but also surprised at how comfortable I immediately felt with her.

"Su, this may sound a little strange," she said, "but if I give you my number, will you call me?"

I was completely stunned and gave her a huge smile. "Of course I will!"

"Okay," she said; I handed her one of the two pens I always carried now, and she wrote it down for me. "It's just that my ex is at this party, so I can't really talk to you here, but I'd love to see you."

My eyes grew wide at the delicious delicacy of it all, and I was beaming at the fact that she would make this bold move just to find a way to see me. "Oh, of course," I said, "I'll call you tomorrow!"

"Okay," she said with a coy smile.

"Okay!" I repeated. We hugged again, and she asked me to slip out of the room before she did. At the time, I thought she was being overly dramatic, but the veil of secrecy made it even more exciting. As I came back to the kitchen, I was smiling from ear to ear. Markus had seen me slip into the room and he was looking up at me with a curious expression.

"What's going on?" he asked in a half-whisper once I had come near enough to not be overheard.

"Oh nothing," I lied, "Are you about ready to go?" I was bursting with the news and couldn't wait to tell him; I also wanted to avoid the awkwardness of seeing Kay now that we had made this plan.

"Sure," he said, "let me just finish my beer," and I waited for a few interminable minutes while he did so. We walked down the stairs, saying goodbye to the woman we had met on the street out front, who was still smoking by the door.

"Okay," Markus said once we were out of earshot, "What's going on?"

I told him the story and he was almost as floored as I was.

"What are you going to do?" he said.

"Well I'll call her of course!"

"I wonder who her ex was," Markus went on, stroking his chin, "it couldn't have been the women I was talking to in the kitchen; they were in a couple. I can't actually remember seeing anyone who wasn't in a couple except for the woman you were talking to."

"Well what difference does it make," I said curtly, not wanting to dwell on her ex.

"Oh!" Markus said with a smile, "Maybe it was *Jen*!" and we both laughed, finally reaching the T station and on our way home.

I was more smitten than I had realized. Her eyes, her smile, the glances we exchanged, the way she beckoned me into that room and asked for me to call her, all kept playing and replaying in my head. I had trouble sleeping that night, and though I knew I should wait, I called the very next afternoon. A woman's voice answered the phone.

"Who is this?" she said.

"It's Su; could I speak to Kay, please?"

"She's not home," the voice said gruffly.

"Could I leave a message for her?" I asked hopefully. There was silence and then a loud sigh on the other end. "Could you just tell her Su called?" I pleaded, "My number is xxx-xxxx"

"OK," she said and abruptly hung up.

Something didn't seem quite right. For the rest of the day I worried about whether I had taken the wrong tone or hadn't been sufficiently courteous or made some other misstep that could have caused this person to have that reaction. As the hours went on, I began to worry that because of that unpleasant interchange, the message wouldn't be relayed to Kay. I toyed with the idea of calling her again, but knew I shouldn't; at the least I had to wait a couple of days. "But she wants to hear from me!" I kept telling myself, "and I told her I'd call her today!" Had I screwed up this incredible story with just one bad phone call?

I had planned to wait longer but I called again the very next day. To my great relief, it was Kay who answered the phone this time.

"Oh hi, Su!" she said brightly.

We chatted for a while and all my usual anxiety melted away; we arranged to get a drink together the following weekend. I gave her my number in case she needed to get in touch and we talked for a while longer before saying goodbye. I was ecstatic; something about Kay was so very different from every woman

I'd dated before. Was it the story? Was it the ease I felt talking to her? Was it her ready and lovely smile? I had no idea, but I knew I couldn't wait to see her.

I could barely concentrate that week and when Friday came, I left work early to give myself time to prepare and calm my nerves. We had decided to meet for a drink at the Kendall Café, and I got there early in the hopes of calming my pre-date jitters before she arrived. To my surprise, she was already there, and as soon as I saw her my anxiety disappeared once again; we chatted and flirted as though we'd known each other for months. We had a couple of drinks each and walked back to the T stop together; I would get off at Harvard Square and she would continue on to Davis. I wanted so much to kiss her or even hold her hand but I wasn't ready to ask for either yet; instead I just managed to ask her if she wanted to hang out again sometime soon.

"And what would we do next time?" she said with her coy smile and a twinkle in her eye.

I was caught off-guard. "Well, maybe we could go dancing?" I asked, raising my voice at the end in an uncertain question.

"Yes!" she said enthusiastically, "I would like that!"

With that, we had reached my stop; we hugged each other tightly and I waved as her train pulled away from the station. As usual I did a thorough critique of my performance on the date. It ended well, and I asked her out again, and she agreed: *that was good.* I didn't try to hold her hand or kiss her, so maybe she thought we were just hanging out as friends: *that was bad.* But she gave me her number and asked me to call her – clearly, she's interested: *that's good.* But maybe now she thinks *I'm* not interested in *her* in that way: *that's bad.* But the hug felt like more than just a friendly hug: *that's good.* But it *was* just a hug: *that's bad.* When she asked what we would do if we hung out again, she was probably looking for clarity about my interest, and I just asked her to "hang out:" *that's bad, very bad.* I went on and on like this for pretty much the rest of the night.

I managed to wait a couple of days before I called her again, now anxious that I had to get things on the right track and make it clear that I was very much interested in her. Once again, another woman's voice answered the phone.

"Hello?" the voice said.

"Hi, this is Su, may I speak to Kay please?" I asked, hoping for a better response than last time.

"No, she's not here. And she shouldn't be hanging out with you anyway," she said and hung up abruptly.

I was shocked. What could her roommates possibly have against me? I waited a day and then called again, now hanging up if I didn't hear Kay on the other end. This went on for more than a week, and I was growing desperate; eventually I left a message again, and despite grumbling about it, the woman answering the phone did take it down.

Days went by with no word from Kay; I was miserable thinking I wouldn't be able to see her again. I called less and less often (though still far too much), never reaching her on the phone. The next weekend came around and I went to a few parties with Markus, half-heartedly engaging with people, and somehow ended up with the phone number of a lovely young woman named Leila who managed a coffeeshop in a nearby town. I was having a hard time thinking about anything but Kay, but Markus and other friends convinced me I should give Leila a call. She was extremely enthusiastic on the phone, and we set up a date for the following Friday.

The next week wore on uneventfully, and while I still was pining after Kay it was becoming more and more clear that I was not going to see her again. I began to get excited about Leila, and by Friday I was looking forward to our date. I didn't feel particularly nervous, perhaps because I was still thinking about Kay, but I thought it would be a good experience and help me shake off this obsession. Just as I was about to leave my place to see Leila, the phone rang.

"Su?" the familiar voice said.

"KAY!" I said, unable to hide my excitement and surprise.

A Friend of Jen's

"Hi Su! I'm so sorry it took so long to get back to you, I was on a trip and my roommates can be really bad about messages."

"Oh, that's totally ok!" I said, just relieved to be hearing from her. I wanted so much to talk to her but I also didn't want to make Leila wait, so I got over my usual fears and asked, "do you want to meet up sometime soon?"

"Yes!" she replied, "How about tomorrow night? I can't go dancing but maybe we could get some food together?"

"That would be wonderful!" I said. We quickly came up with a plan and I raced out the door to meet Leila.

Leila was both more lovely and more interested in me than I had remembered, but I was extremely distracted by thoughts of Kay. We had a drink and started walking around Harvard Square. All I could think about was Kay and what would happen tomorrow.

At some point I remember Leila saying, "So, you were saying you live near here, right? Is one of these buildings yours?" and though it was, I mumbled something about how I actually lived on the other side of the square. "Oh, I see, do you want to walk over there? I, um, don't have to work early tomorrow..."

At this point even I was able to understand what she was getting at, but my mind was far too filled with thoughts of Kay for it to matter. All I wanted to do was end this date so I could get home and plan for tomorrow. I walked her back to her car and we hugged goodbye; Leila was clearly disappointed, and while part of me felt regret at not being able to connect with her, for the most part I was just relieved I could finally get home and start preparing mentally for my date with Kay.

The next day passed in a blur of anxious preparation, not doing anything tangible but mostly worrying about what was to come. When we finally met at a restaurant in Kenmore Square, we again fell into our warm connection and all the worries drifted away. I asked her why her roommate had said she shouldn't be hanging out with me, and she laughed and said that since she was bisexual and her roommates were all lesbians, they got upset every time she dated a boy.

"But they can't tell me who to date," she said with the coy smile and eye wrinkles that I had longed for all those days.

I didn't understand the logic of why her friends would have an opinion on her sexual preferences, but it hardly mattered to me – I was absolutely elated. She had made it clear it was a date, we were having a great time, and all was well. As we took the train home, I finally asked her if I could kiss her.

"Mmmm... not *yet*," she said with an exceptionally brilliant smile. "Maybe next time," tossing her curls.

"Okay, I can wait," I said, smiling as well. She had made her intentions clear, as had I; a kiss was on the way, and it seemed like things couldn't be better. I took one more step: "Since it's hard to get a hold of you, do you want to just call me?" I asked.

"Sure," she said enthusiastically, "I'll call you next week!"

Everything seemed perfect. I went home extremely happy with how the date had gone with none of the usual self-doubt, falling into a deep and sound sleep. A couple of nights ago, I had thought I had lost Kay for good, but now things were shaping up better than I could have expected, and *she* was going to call *me* so I would no longer have to deal with her unfriendly roommates.

I went into the next week with a spring in my step, expecting a call from her any day, but not overly worried at first when I didn't hear from her. By Wednesday I was surprised she hadn't called me, as I was sure she'd give me a day or two of notice if we were going to go out that weekend. By Friday, I was a little panicked, and though I had put off making plans to make sure I'd have time to see her, I ended up going out with Markus once it was clear she wouldn't call that night. By Saturday evening, I was feeling desolate, and by the following Monday I was a wreck.

Eventually I started calling her again, but fell into the same cycle as before – I would call, her roommates would answer, and I would never get a call back. Given what she told me about her roommates, I wondered whether they were even relaying the messages to her, so I would call again and again, at least once a day for more than a week, until at some point I again began to accept that she might not call again.

Despite the small number of actual interactions we'd had, it took me more than a little while to get over Kay. For weeks every time the phone would ring I would jump, thinking it would be her again, but of course it never was. Every time I was in Davis Square I thought that I might run into her somewhere, but I never did. Soon days became weeks and weeks became months; as much as I would never forget the magical moments we spent together, I knew I had to move on. My friends couldn't understand why I was so hung up on someone I barely knew, and frankly, it was hard for me to understand as well. Something about our connection had been different in a way I had never experienced before, and all I knew is that I was desperate to explore it further.

After a few months had passed I again became certain I would never see her again, but as with most things concerning Kay, I was wrong. Nearly a year later, I ran into her at the Diesel Café near Porter Square. I had just walked in as she was walking out with her coffee. She stopped in her tracks and gave me the wide smile I had missed so much.

"Su!" she said brightly.

By this point I had grown somewhat bitter about the whole experience, but seeing her made all of that melt away. I felt all the warmth I had felt for her returning to my head and heart, breaking into a wide smile.

"How are you?" I asked, genuinely happy to see her.

"I'm good, I'm good..." she continued, trailing off her words as her eyes searched my face and body from top to bottom. "Wow I'm just *so attracted* to you," she said, almost to herself, and then broke into her big smile again. "Sorry, I have to go, but it was *so good* see you!"

I didn't know what to say, floored both by seeing her and her comment. How could she be that attracted to me but not want to spend time with me? I wanted to ask her to hang out again but given what had happened before I didn't want to risk the waiting and rejection again. I resolved to stay silent, but was surprised to hear myself blurting out "Call me!" as she walked away. She blew me a kiss as she walked out the door.

That was the last time I would see her in Cambridge, but decades later, by sheer coincidence, we now live in the same city again. I ran into her on the street a few years after moving here: we were both surprised to see each other and said a quick hello before we hurried off to our respective destinations. We added each other on social media at that time; she had married a wonderful man and had two beautiful children.

To this day, we sometimes send each other messages and "like" each other's photos. Now divorced, she still occasionally remarks on how beautiful I am, and it feels nice, but the intense feelings I once had for her are long gone.

Every few years, she'll ask if we can meet up for a drink, saying that we have so much to catch up on. I always enthusiastically agree, but something inevitably comes up – one of her kids gets sick, there's a snowstorm, one of us has a flat tire. At this point it has become almost comical: even when we have a concrete plans I've learned to wait to find out what unexpected event will foil it this time, sometimes less than an hour before we plan to meet. I always chuckle to myself when it happens – our inability to meet is almost as improbable as our initial meeting. I bear no ill will for everything that has happened; I have only warm feelings for her and am thankful for her presence in my journey.

I do believe there is a reason we appeared in one another's lives, despite the stars deciding that we were only to admire each other from afar. Kay had seen something in me that many other women had not, and I had felt an ease with her that was unexpected, oddly reminding me of the women I'd met as "Kitty" on the chat line years before. Looking back, I realize that she was the first bisexual woman I would feel this mutual attraction and rapport with, but far from the last.

Two Secrets

When Markus left to go back to Sweden, he left a substantial hole in my life. He was my first best friend since high school, and I didn't realize just how much time we spent together and how much his presence meant to me until he was no longer there. Though I still traveled in the same circles after he left, the parties began to feel like the same event repeated over and over again with a slightly different set of people in a slightly different venue.

There were parties thrown by a socialite who lived in an entire floor of the Charles Hotel where a Kennedy once made an appearance (I didn't talk to him, but everyone made sure to point him out), wild art-themed events in an old house organized by a friend who busked as an eight-foot tall silent bride in Harvard Square, loft parties in makeshift studios in the industrial area near South Station (before they became fancy condos), and even a naked party or two which in conservative Boston felt like the height of debauchery. None of them held my interest, though; I had lost a deep connection and was desperately looking for something to replace it with.

Having more time on my own, I started working on my music again in earnest, a passion I had mostly put on hold while Markus had been around. I had been writing songs since I was twelve or so, and over time had come to think of it as a more and more important part of my life. In those days, I still harbored the fantasy that all my engineering and science education was just a "backup plan;" my true destiny was to be a pop star. The few friends who had heard my songs had always liked them (though I can't remember anyone enthusiastically asking for more), so around the time I started my graduate work I had submitted an entry to a national songwriting contest. The song got reasonable marks ("average radio quality"), which I generously interpreted as meaning my music was ready for a national audience.

After Markus left, I put together a small set of songs I had been writing and performing at open mics, releasing it as small album on an independent artists' site that had launched the careers of a few well-known bands. It took tireless nights of writing, recording, and re-recording, and while I hated the isolation and time away from friends, especially with Markus gone, I was proud of what I had created.

I was so certain that I would be an overnight success I waited until after a major deadline had passed to release it, expecting

Two Secrets

I'd need an open calendar to deal with the press and tons of fan mail that were sure to come. When I released the album, I didn't tell a soul – I figured they would hear about it when it became incredibly popular (overnight) and then ask me about it – "Wait, this is *you*?" they would ask, incredulously. I would smile coyly and admit that indeed it was.

The reality turned out to be very different from my expectations. I released it on a Friday night, and checked a few hours later to see how many downloads I had received. I was shocked to see it was zero – surely, I thought, the counter must be broken. I did a test download onto my own computer, and went back to the counter – it now stood at one. I figured perhaps it would just take a while before people would notice it, so I waited until the next morning, and sadly the counter was still at one. Feeling my dream begin to slip away, I desperately started emailing friends and colleagues, at first dozens and then hundreds of people, feeling a growing dismay when even after a month the counter barely made it past a hundred. The overconfident part of me blamed the lack of promotion and advertising and the "music racket," but the more practical part of me began to accept that perhaps my music was not quite the pop sensation I had always imagined it to be.

In the months afterwards, I would send the tracks to anyone who showed any interest at all, and one of those people was

Trix, a recent Wellesley senior who had started working in our lab as a research assistant. She was a DJ at her college radio station and offered to play one of my songs on the air (the only radio play I've ever received, as far as I know), and afterwards asked if I'd be interested in jamming with her and her friends.

"You have a band?" I asked.

"Well, not a band exactly," she laughed, "but we do enjoy getting together to play music."

"Sure!" I said, thankful to find some avenue to keep playing music that wouldn't be so isolating.

After my humbling album release the thought of investing endless additional hours on my music alone didn't hold much appeal; furthermore, I had experienced some truly joyful experiences playing music with others in the past, so I was happy to give it a try.

That Sunday I showed up with my electric guitar at Trix's rented Somerville house, where she lived with Adina, who was also a member of the band. Anaisha arrived shortly afterwards, a poet and writer who would eventually become a lifelong friend. Trix and Adina were accomplished musicians – Trix played both electric guitar and saxophone, while Adina was well-versed in jazz piano. Anaisha didn't play any instruments but was interested in writing lyrics and wanted to be involved, so we gave her some drum sticks and a basic digital drum machine to make up the rhythm section.

Before I even unzipped my guitar case Trix said, "Wait – before we play, we drink!" She pulled out some bottles of cheap wine, and we all toasted each other and chatted for a good half hour. Eventually, we connected up our instruments, started playing some chords, and got a few grooves going; I felt a real connection to this group of women and could see myself doing this every Sunday for a while.

Just as we were getting comfortable playing together, we heard someone noisily coming through the door.

"Stella!" Trix said, looking around.

"STELLA!!!" they all shouted in unison.

Stella burst into the room with her gigantic electric-acoustic bass, and yelled "WHAT?" with her wild, wide smile, sending everyone into fits of laughter.

Stella was tall and lanky, with a short bleached-blond buzz cut, bright blue eyes, ripped jeans, and a sleeveless tank with lovely tufts of hair visible when she raised her arms. I was both instantly smitten with her and also absolutely certain she was only interested in other women. Still, I couldn't help but try to get her attention.

The first couple of jam sessions she barely paid any attention to me – she wouldn't laugh at my corny jokes and would only give me cursory replies, but after a couple of months she began to warm up to me and we would talk and laugh together like old friends. The Sunday sessions were more social gatherings than formal jam sessions – we would start with wine, play for an hour or so, then curl up together on the couch to watch the Simpsons or a movie.

Over time, Trix and Adina felt like we should be more serious about our music, so we came up with a band name, started rearranging our grooves into songs, made lead sheets, and began referring to our Sunday afternoons as "band practice." At the same time, we started spending time together outside of these sessions – we would go to parties and dinners together and would sometimes forego a jam session when someone really needed to talk about something that was happening in their life. I was delighted to have a wonderful new group of close friends; it wasn't the same as Markus, but while losing a best friend I felt like I had gained a family.

There was just one problem – my attraction to Stella, despite all intentions, continued to grow. I would sometimes be tempted to ask her to hang out on our own, but I was worried that the near-certain rejection would disrupt my newfound musical family. I both valued my closeness with them and feared being thrown back into isolation, so I never acted on my impulses, pining for her in silence.

Eventually, after playing with the group for about five months, it happened unintentionally: I brought up a party on an upcoming Saturday late in February that I thought the group would like. Trix, Adina, and Anaisha were all interested but had conflicts that night. "I'll go with you," Stella said, and just like that, without even trying, a date was set. The party was near my apartment, so we planned to meet at my place, have a couple of drinks, and then head over.

Stella came over, hair styled up with pomade and in stunning red vinyl pants, and suddenly we were both nervous. We had never hung out with only each other, and the reality of the situation made us both tongue-tied. After a couple of drinks, we were talking a little more freely, and started getting ready to go to the party. Stella asked if she could leave her bag at my place, and not getting the hint, I asked how she would get it at the end of the night.

She gave me a strange look and said, "just bring it to band practice tomorrow!"

"Oh, right, that makes sense!" I said, and we headed out.

All I remember about the party was that it was loud, the music was great, and neither of us knew anyone. We ended up dancing together, at first just near each other, but soon closer and closer until we were holding each other as we moved. We shared our first kiss on the dance floor, which lasted for much longer than either of us expected.

Our bodies stayed in continuous contact for the next few songs, and eventually Stella pulled herself back enough to ask, "Do you want to go back to your place?"

I immediately agreed and we walked the few blocks home holding hands.

As we were going up the elevator, she said, "One thing though."

"What?" I said.

"We can't have sex, I'm on my period," she said frankly, looking right at me.

"Oh, sure, no problem!" I said.

She probably expected that I'd be disappointed, and may have been surprised at my lack of reaction, but after all the time that had gone by and the angst I'd felt over my masculinity, I was very relieved to not have to face all those demons on that first night. We'd also both had a lot to drink and were ready to just go to sleep.

We peeled ourselves out of our outfits and curled up together on my queen-sized futon; it was the first time I'd slept with someone since Kate and the first time ever in my own bed. Though this time it had happened much more suddenly than with Kate, it felt wonderful to be with Stella and I went to sleep happier than I had been in a long time. We both woke up hung over, late in the morning, and realized we were due at band practice in less than an hour.

"I don't think we can make it in time," she said, "at least not without food, and I need food and coffee or I won't be able to *deal*."

"I don't think they'll mind if we're a little late," I said.

"But if we come in late... together..." she said, her voice trailing off in implication.

"Oh..." I said, not having thought about this. "Do you think it will cause drama?" I asked.

While the potential for drama is what had kept me from asking her out in the first place, I had assumed it would be because she would reject me. I had never considered that we might end up dating, and that this in itself could cause a problem. Now I was worrying about it too.

"No – I mean yes – I mean I don't know," she said, bursting out laughing. "Whatever, we're all adults," she said dismissively, back to the tough-as-nails Stella I had come to adore. Instantly my fears were put to rest as well. We had a leisurely breakfast nearby, picked up her bass at her apartment, and went to practice.

Everyone was already there when we arrived, and Trix and Anaisha gave us a knowing look as if they already knew what was going on. They didn't say anything, though, and we just plugged in our instruments and joined the practice session without incident. Afterwards, we curled up on the couch for the Simpsons as usual, though Stella and I sat cuddled up next to each other; still, nobody said a thing – we were family.

Stella and I made plans to see each other again the following Friday; we had dinner in Central Square, then came back to my place and headed right to my room.

"Guess what?" she said.

"What?" I asked.

"My period is over!" she said in a singsong voice with a smile.

We started making out, quickly taking off all our clothes, our hands all over each other, when she asked, "do you have a condom?"

"I do," I said; I had bought my first box ever after our previous night together. I pulled one out from the bedside shelf, and she caressed me as I opened the wrapper. As I started to unroll it and put it on, I could feel myself shuddering, and she could too.

"You're shivering," she said, concerned.

"I'm fine," I said, trying to shake it off, and tried to slip the condom over my fast-fading erection, but in moments it was clear it was not going to work.

"What's wrong?" she asked, and in my embarrassment and terror, I broke down in tears.

"This is my first time, and I thought it would be fine, but I think I just have a lot of hang-ups about it now, and I just don't think I'm ready." I buried my face in my chest, expecting the worst.

Stella, though, was unexpectedly gentle. "Don't worry about it, it's fine," she said in a comforting voice, "if you're not ready for sex, we don't have to have sex, come here," she said, drawing my body towards hers.

I was still curled up, in tears, but she drew me to her warm body and held me. We fell asleep that way, and I woke up with her arms still enveloping me, still embarrassed but happy that she was still there. I expected she'd have the same reaction as Kate afterwards and that I'd never see her again, but I was glad she had at least stayed to hold me through the night.

Stella, though, was far more patient and kind than I ever could have expected. Week after week, night after night, she would work on me, caressing me, playing with me, teasing me, letting me become more and more familiar with her and her body, being naked in her presence, having an erection while we embraced. After a month of this slow guidance, she asked me for a condom again; this time unrolling it onto my cock herself. To my surprise, this time it made my erection only stronger than it had been. She laid back in my bed, I rubbed some KY jelly onto her vulva, and entered her body for the first time.

The thrill of my first moments inside her was electric, the culmination of all the dreams of sex I'd carried with me since childhood. In mind I felt myself thinking, "I'm finally doing it!" The condom, though, had reduced the sensation more than I expected – I was too inexperienced to know I should have lubricated the inside, or at least made sure there was no air trapped in the tip. At this point I had read countless questionable books and articles about the best ways to pleasure a woman, but unfortunately had never spent the time to understand how to use condoms properly or even read the instructions inside the box.

I started off controlling myself with long, slow strokes as I had read about, feeling the sensations build up in my body. After a few moments I heard a "pop" sound and didn't think anything of it, but suddenly the sensations in my body were far stronger than before. "I must be doing something right," I thought to myself – suddenly it felt incredible to be inside her;

Two Secrets

I felt every part of my body was connected to every part of hers, with intense sensations of pleasure lighting up every inch of my skin. I moved faster and faster, feeling my legs and hips take over from my conscious brain. My body soared to a climax of motion, and then, with a rush of intensity, I felt myself come in a shuddering orgasm, as powerful as the first one I'd had with the yellow bean bag years ago.

I pulled my penis out and instantly realized where the "pop" had come from. The remains of the condom were wrinkled around the base of my penis, the head fully exposed and glistening with cum.

"Stella…" I said, my voice full of anxiety.

"What?" she said, noticing the alarm in my voice.

"The condom broke," I said, nearly in tears.

To this day I will never forget the calm with which Stella dealt with the situation. "Oh, really?" she said, as if it were a minor nuisance. "Well, I'll go to the doctor tomorrow, and she'll give me a morning after pill, and it will be fine!" she said.

"It will?" I said, my mind already imagining having to drop out of school to support a child, the rest of my future dictated by this one mistake.

"Yes," she said, "it will be fine, Su, don't worry," and comforted *me*, despite my being the cause of all of this. I was certain it was extremely stressful for her as well, but she hid her stress to make sure I was OK.

We took the T towards her place to have lunch together, and she headed for home as I went back to my lab. She again assured me everything would be all right. I went to work, racked with anxiety about the situation, and would have a hard time focusing for the next few days. Stella kept me up to date on the first and second application of high-dose synthetic progesterone (this was before the "one-step" version of Plan B), but I continued to worry.

We made plans to see each other the next weekend, and as she arrived at my place I felt super-nervous about having sex, but as soon as she came in the door she sang, "Guess who got her peeeeriooooood!!" with a big smile, and we both laughed and hugged in relief. Seeing how relieved she was I realized how stressed she had been about this as well, and how much she had protected me from all of those worries.

After that first harrowing experience, we began to have sex every time we were together. For years afterwards, though, I would be unwilling to ejaculate during sex even while wearing a condom, afraid of another accident, substantially reducing my sexual pleasure with a new form of anxiety. Still, we had many wonderful nights exploring each others' bodies and getting to know each other intimately. In my mind, sex became a means of extreme closeness and intimacy, but separated from the physical sensation of an orgasm. I knew many ways to make myself cum through masturbation and had become extremely proficient at giving myself pleasure; it wasn't necessary for that to occur while I was being close with Stella. I valued those naked moments with her for what they were, a time to be closer to another human being than I had ever been.

After about six months together, when we had become far more comfortable with each other, she started to ask me more personal questions, trying to break through the shell I kept around my inner thoughts. One night, with our arms wrapped around each other's naked bodies, she gently said, "Su, tell me something about you that I don't know."

I knew exactly what she meant, but I tried deflecting the question by talking about silly things or my research; she wasn't having any of it. "No," she said, grabbing my shoulders and looking me in the eyes, "something really personal, about *you*," she insisted.

"Well," I said cautiously, "I guess... I have two really deep and dark secrets."

"What?" she said, sitting up in the bed and opening her eyes wide, "What kind of secrets?"

"Oh, nothing that hurt anyone," I said quickly.

"Ha! I know *that*," she laughed good naturedly.

"They're just things that no one else can know."

"Oh, c'mon, not even me?" she said, and pried and pleaded gently and with loving pokes, until I finally gave in.

"OK, I'll tell you ONE." I said.

"OK," she said, sounding a little disappointed. "What is it?"

I hemmed and hawed for some time, and eventually said in a quiet voice, "I like the feeling of having things in my butt," and immediately turned away buried my face in the pillow.

"That's all?" she laughed. "A lot of people like that!"

"No!" I said. "It's weird."

"It's not weird, silly, it's fine!" she said.

Once again she put her warm arms around me, put her mouth right up to me ear, and said in a whispered voice, "You mean something like this?" as she started softly stroking my bottom, sliding her finger between my cheeks and stroking my anus.

Embarrassed, I wanted to ask her to stop, but instead, I felt an "mmmmm" inadvertently escape my mouth, my bottom twitching a little bit. It felt wonderful, and I wanted more, but was afraid to ask for it.

Over the next few weeks, without my saying a word, Stella slowly became more and more bold, eventually putting a little lube on her finger and putting it inside me. I loved it and she loved my reactions; at first she would just gently stroke me while she had her finger there, but soon she would venture there while we had sex as well. I was still unwilling to cum while I was inside her, even with the condom on, but those moments with her finger inside me were truly blissful, and something I had never expected to experience with a female partner. Eventually I would tell her everything about this part of me – the butt plugs, the yellow bean bag, and even the weight bench.

As weeks grew into months, she kept pressing me for the second secret.

"No," I said, "I can't tell you that one."

"Why?" she asked.

"Because it's bad, it's really bad," I said, turning away in shame.

"Oh c'mon, Su, what could it be?" she asked crossly.

This went on for some number of weeks until I finally relented; I told her all about calling the chat lines as Kitty and masturbating while I talked to men.

"WOW!" she said, her eyes growing wide again, and I curled up into a little ball of shame again. "No, Su, it's nothing to be ashamed of, it's incredible!"

She went on to ask me a lot of questions about the experience that I had not thought of myself – how it made me feel, why it turned me on, what kind of men I liked talking to. I wasn't ready to think about all of this, though, so as quickly as I could I changed the topic of conversation and we never brought it up it again.

That conversation opened a certain door, though; we started talking about sex and sexuality much more openly: what we found attractive, what felt good and not good, what turned us on. I eventually told her how when I had met her I had assumed she only dated women, that I had been incredibly attracted to her but didn't think I had a chance.

"Really?" she asked, looking thoughtfully into the distance. "I mean, I've dated women before, but I've mostly dated boys."

"Sometimes," I said quietly, looking down, "I feel kind of like I'm a lesbian trapped in a man's body."

Though I loved to joke around with her, I said this with a straight face, completely serious. She looked at me, eyes narrowing at first, but then understanding that this was a moment of vulnerability, not a joke.

"You know," she said slowly, "a lot of guys say that as a joke, and it really pisses me off, but with you, I think it' s actually true." Neither of us said anything for a while; the weight of that insight silenced us both, and in many ways it weighs on me still.

After a year of spending almost every weekend night together, Stella and I started to drift apart. We always used to joke that we weren't the right people for each other in the long term, and while for that first year it was hard to keep us apart, the truth of that joke started to surface. We would still see each other, but less and less often, sometimes skipping the sex just to hold each other through the night. One of the last times we saw each other was near my birthday; she handed me a gift bag containing a stuffed bear and a small yellow pillow.

"Thank you!" I said, a little confused.

"Don't you get it?" she asked? I didn't, and after dropping a few hints she spelled it out for me.

"It's a PANDA BEAR and a YELLOW BEAN BAG," she said, rolling her eyes. Of course: my first bedmate and my first lover. Stella had become both for me, but now that we were growing apart the moment felt bittersweet. I hugged her and thanked her for her sweet gift, feeling an unexpected sadness, as though a chapter in our lives was coming to a close.

I will be forever grateful to Stella. I wonder sometimes where I would be today without her steady patience, her calm acceptance of my strangeness, her loving and persistent encouragement to break through all of those barriers of shame, inadequacy, and uncertain masculinity. I've tried to reach out to her over the years – we met once in Cambridge when I came back to visit, and then once at her parents' home (ironically, a suburb of my current city), but since then my messages and friend requests have gone unanswered. I was not as available to her as I could have been once we stopped seeing each other, even as a friend, and to this day I regret not nurturing that connection even after the romantic part had melted away.

There are nights when I think through all of my lovers, making sure I can remember, imagine, and feel gratitude for each one and the part they've played in my journey. The chain has always begun with Stella; it will forevermore begin with Stella.

Do You Think We're Lucky?

"Now lie back," Ji said.

"Right here, in the sand?" I asked, already a little worried about sand getting on my carefully selected date outfit. She had brought me to this industrial-looking beach in South Boston and somehow convinced me to sit down with her in the sand despite our fancy clothes.

"Yes, c'mon!" She leaned back and pulled me down with her. "Isn't this nice?" she asked.

It was early in the evening in late June, the sky was just beginning to break into the warm colors of sunset, and a light breeze was coming off the water.

"Yes," I had to admit, "It is nice."

"Okay now HERE IT COMES!" she yelled.

Out of nowhere, a giant passenger jet that had been a speck in the sky a moment ago came down directly on top of us (or so it seemed); as it zoomed over we could feel the turbulence of its wake, the heat from its engines, and see every last detail of its fuselage. I was stunned into silence, and when it passed, she started laughing at my expression, and I couldn't help but laugh too.

"What was that?" I gasped.

"The airport is right over there," she said, pointing behind us; "this is right on their runway path."

"Wow!" I cried, still laughing.

We talked and laughed on the leisurely walk back to the T station. It felt like it was going well: we were flirting, both laughing, and her hand would brush close to mine again and again – I kept wanting to intertwine my fingers in hers, but it was our first date and I didn't want to seem too forward. She asked if it would be ok to stop at her place so she could check her messages. After a brief conversation there we awkwardly said our goodbyes there and I took the train home, wondering if I had said something wrong.

I had met Ji on a personals site; I was immediately drawn to her slender form and androgynous style, as well as her artfully crafted profile text that gave only surface clues to her underlying mysteries. She was a master's student in a film school in

Boston, looking for interesting people to talk to, and when I wrote to her she wrote back almost immediately. We chatted very briefly online before arranging our first date, this walk near her home. She was even more attractive to me than I had expected from her photos, and I was already thinking about when I should call her again and what I should suggest for our next date, assuming I hadn't screwed up our first date too badly.

Almost as soon as I got home, the phone rang; it was Ji. "Oh hi, Ji, I had such a great time with you tonight!" I said in my cookie-cutter post-date follow-up.

"You did?" she said, skeptically.

Uh-oh, I thought.

"Do you think I'm attractive?" she asked bluntly.

My heart raced, thinking of the fateful night when Kate had asked me that question after I had completely missed her advances.

"Of course I think you're attractive!" I said quickly.

"Wait, sorry," she said, "I still get the English wrong sometimes." I could hear her thumbing through a book. "Do you *find me* attractive?"

I was blushing at this point. "I do, Ji, I really do!"

"Really?" she said, still sounding skeptical.

"Why are you asking, Ji?" I asked, perplexed.

"Well...," she said hesitatingly, "Didn't you notice I wore a skirt?"

Of course I had noticed; it was a tiny, lacy, bouncy multi-layered affair that it took all my willpower not to stare at. It was particularly challenging on the way back to her place as she kept brushing her bottom to get the sand out. I had definitely noticed.

"I wore that because I also wore this special underwear tonight, I don't know what you call it, it's like a triangle with a string in the back..." she trailed off, searching for the right word.

"A thong?" I asked.

"Yes," she said brightly, "a thong! I wore that tonight, and you didn't even see it!" she said in a whine.

I could tell that she was half-serious and half-teasing, and tried my best to play along. "I really would have liked to see it, and perhaps I could see it on a different occasion?" I asked, overly formal in my nervousness.

"Perhaps," she said skeptically, but there was a smile in her voice.

Do You Think We're Lucky?

I racked my brain for possibilities. "How about the 4th of July? Do you want to watch the fireworks on the banks of the Charles?"

"But doesn't the whole city get crazy after that, where you can't get a train or a cab?" she asked.

"It does," I said, "But I live close enough that we could walk over here, have some drinks, and hang out until things die down again."

"*Hang out?*" she said, again half-serious and half-teasing.

"Sure!" I said, laughing, "and other things."

"And other things," she repeated drily. "Well, I'll have to check my calendar," she said, and while I had thought things were going well before this point, I suddenly feared she was not going to go for it.

"I'm just kidding," she continued, and then with mock formality mimicking my own, "Yes, I would be honored to see the fireworks with you, and then *hang out,*" emphasizing the final words in a way that made us both laugh.

The night of the 4th came, and we met at the Kendall T to walk over to the Cambridge side of the Charles. The view wouldn't be quite as good as the Boston side, but it would be far easier to escape the crowds and head to my place afterwards. She wore a close-fitting t-shirt and tiny shorts, and I found myself even more attracted to her before, though I was concerned since her outfit was less date-like that she might be sending a signal about her intentions. My fears soon melted away - we sat shoulder to shoulder during the event, and when I reached for her hand she reached out to meet it enthusiastically. We held hands with our arms interlocked for most of the show, stroking each others' forearms with our hands, and I was happy with how things were progressing.

As soon as we heard the last strains of the 1812 Overture, marking the end of the fireworks, we got up and started walking up Massachusetts Avenue. We looked behind us and could see the crowd of hundreds of thousands slowly heading towards us (and all other directions), slowly decompressing from the event like an army of drunken zombies. We walked as fast as we could to stay ahead of the swell, and after twenty minutes of walk-running we were across the street from my building with most of the crowd behind us.

"Is there a drugstore near here?" she asked, looking around furtively.

"Yeah, there's one right here, but it's closed because of the 4th."

"Oh," she said, disappointed.

"What do you need?" I asked, mentally taking an inventory of my well-stocked medicine cabinet.

Do You Think We're Lucky?

"Oh, nothing, it's not that important." She was peering into glass of the closed store, holding my hand, and asked, "Do you think we're lucky?"

"Well yes," I said, blushing, "I think I'm very lucky to be here with you."

She laughed and said, "You're sweet, but that's not what I meant. Let's go."

We went upstairs to my apartment, and I made us some gin and tonics. We talked and laughed awkwardly for a little while and then almost in a single fluid motion, we put down our drinks and leaned in for our first kiss. That kiss turned quickly into many more kisses and caresses, and soon I got up, reached for her hand, and walked with her to my bedroom. Closing the door behind us, we continued to kiss and touch each other, rapidly pulling off the minimal layers we'd worn for that hot summer night.

Her lovely, slender body had been mostly visible through her thin t-shirt, but when I pulled it over her head and slipped off her bra I was in for a surprise. Her chest was even less pronounced than mine, her two nipples erect against a smooth surface pulled taut against her ribs. At that moment I realized I didn't know what I would find when I took off her shorts and panties. I was also completely certain that it didn't matter to me. I was incredibly turned on by her, and wanted to feel the entirety of her body against mine, whatever that might mean.

As I slid her panties off and caught my first sight of her lovely vulva, I was slightly surprised but not disappointed. She had pulled off my pants as well and I was lying on my back, fully erect, with her on top of me.

"Just let me grab a condom," I said.

"Aw, why?" she whined.

"It's safer," I responded, surprised.

"Oh, you Americans," she said. "Fine."

I slipped it on and she slid her already wet vulva over the shaft and tip as she made an "mmmmm" sound that reminded me of my own vocalizations when my bottom was being stimulated. In a single motion, she reached down with her hand and slipped me inside her, pushing back against my chest to take all of me inside. She was holding my chest and rocking back and forth, her eyes closed and moaning with pleasure. My eyes were wide, unable to take my eyes off this beautiful, sexy being I was lucky enough to be with.

Suddenly I happened to look down and saw blood all over my thighs. "Oh no!" I cried.

"AHHHHHH!" she wailed.

Do You Think We're Lucky?

My first thought was that my penis had somehow damaged her tiny body and that she was now bleeding internally. "Oh my god, are you ok?" I cried.

"What?" she said, surprised, and then started laughing. "I'm fine, I'm just having my period."

A wave of relief washed over me as I realized I hadn't killed her with my penis, followed by a wave of embarrassment at my naivete. "Ohhhhh..." I said and started laughing as well. Stella never wanted to have sex during her period, so this was an entirely new experience for me. "So *this* is what you meant about 'being lucky.'"

"Yes, of course," she laughed.

"Does it hurt? Do you want to stop?" I asked.

"No, not at all," she said, and she continued to ride my hips, even more vigorously now, coming quickly in a delicious scream of delight.

She slid off me and saw that I was still hard, "You didn't come?" she asked.

"No, I don't usually come with a condom on," I said truthfully, not wanting to reveal my fear of letting go due to that first condom breakage.

"Then I LOSE!" she cried.

"No, you win!" I responded, "I'm glad you came!"

"But I want YOU to come too," she wailed; she seemed genuinely upset, and I consoled her that it was ok, and she seemed somewhat though not completely mollified.

We changed the sheets and made a half-hearted attempt to wash the stains out of the old set in the sink, but we were both exhausted from the night and the intense sex and crawled into bed together. She felt so small and delicate in my arms; she pushed her tiny body deep into the hollow of mine and pulled my arm around her. Even her body temperature seemed to match mine perfectly; I wrapped my other arm around her and fell asleep almost immediately.

The next morning we were hungry for each other again, but she didn't want to stain another pair of sheets, so we decided to wait and just take a shower together. She started playing with me as soon as we got in, and after soaping us both up slipped my hard cock against her vulva, looking down and saying, "I wish I had one of those." Suddenly she turned around and insisted I enter her as she leaned forward against the wall.

"But I don't have a condom," I protested.

"It's fine," she said, "I don't have any diseases, silly."

I was scared, but also incredibly turned on, and I entered her from behind, the first time I'd ever intentionally entered someone with a condom. It felt amazing, but after a few strokes I pulled out, telling her I was afraid I would come. "But that's what I WANT," she said, disappointed. We finished our shower, dried each other off, and after many more kisses eagerly planned our next date.

The next few weeks with Ji were a whirlwind. We would sometimes have dinner or a drink but always head to the bedroom; we couldn't get enough of each other. I had enjoyed having sex with Stella, but I had never hungered for someone like I did for Ji. Our bodies were similarly shaped and seemed to fit together like puzzle pieces; every touch felt electric and even holding her while we slept felt amazing. Though we used condoms, she would continue to be upset about my not coming inside her, saying "it's not FAIR" that she always came but I did not. Those nights turned me on so much that I hardly minded, but she would be genuinely upset that she was not pleasing me in the way she felt she should. The nights I didn't see her, we would talk on the phone, and I would masturbate later thinking about the feeling of her body against mine. The effect she had on me was far-reaching; I even felt more confident about my life and my research, and looked forward to every intense night I would get to spend with her.

About a month in, things took an unexpected turn. I was telling her how I was always thinking about her and wished I could see her every night. She was silent for a moment, and then said, "Well why don't we just move in together?"

I laughed as I thought she was joking, but it became clear she was very serious. "But Ji," I said, "I'm leaving in a couple of months to go to Seattle."

"And what's going to happen to us then?" she asked.

I honestly hadn't thought about it, assuming that I would leave all my Boston connections behind when I left.

"So you're just going to forget about me?" she said, her voice growing angry.

"No, Ji, I'll never forget you, I love you!" I pleaded.

"But then why won't you move in with me?" she protested.

We went on like this for hours until we were both exhausted; it was three in the morning before we hung up. I wasn't really clear on what had happened, and I hoped this would all blow over in the morning.

I was wrong. From that day forward, she would only want to talk about moving in together, I would resist, and we would go back and forth like that for hours. We stopped scheduling dates and didn't see each other at all for a few weeks; one day without warning she showed up at my lab, and my alarmed officemates told me she was asking for me and refused to leave until I talked to her. I walked out to see her, and asked if she would walk with me to a cafe to have lunch; she agreed.

That was the last conversation we would have for many years. We continued to correspond over e-mail, but she couldn't understand why I didn't want to take our relationship to the next level. I had not thought about it seriously before then, and given the intensity of our connection I may have wanted to continue the relationship beyond my time in Boston, but somehow her insistence that we move in together felt like too much too soon, and I ran away.

Eventually the phone calls stopped and we no longer wrote to each other, though ironically by the time I left for Seattle I would have a different girlfriend with whom I persisted a long distance relationship for another year and a half.

Ji and I have kept in touch over the years and we still feel a strong, almost dangerous attraction for each other. Once when she had planned a trip to Seattle, we had plans to meet, but when she told me she hadn't booked a place to stay and was wondering if she could just stay with me I told her it wasn't a good idea and backed out of the plan. I was single at the time, but given our last experience I didn't want to cause further harm to either of us. Since then, we've only stayed in touch from afar.

Decades later, I will never forget the intensity of the nights we spent together, and I stand by my original answer to her question from that 4th of July – I do feel lucky that we had the chance to be together, however briefly it might have been.

An Apple a Day

"GET OFF THE SIDEWALK, ASSHOLE!" a voice yelled as I walked across the Montlake bridge in Seattle, from the University of Washington to the Montlake neighborhood. Startled, I moved to the side, turning to see who was yelling and whether they might be yelling at me. In a familiar red Volkswagen, I saw Sylvia laughing and leaning across the seat, with the passenger-side window rolled down.

"I've been yelling your name for five minutes, and then you finally pay attention when I call you an asshole," she said.

I laughed. "I guess I was just lost in my thoughts."

"Get in," she said, "we're going to my house." I complied; I knew better than to argue with her.

I met Sylvia shortly before things ended with Miko, the long-distance girlfriend I'd been seeing since I left Boston. At the time, I remember being struck by how attracted I was to Sylvia, but kept my distance as I was still trying to make things work with Miko. After a year and a half with thousands of miles between us and no hope of moving to the same city, Miko and I finally called it quits. Within a few weeks of the breakup, I learned through a mutual friend Sam that Sylvia was interested in me. I was both surprised and delighted.

"Are you sure she's interested in *me*?" I asked, perplexed.

"Oh, definitely, she likes guys like you. There was an Indian post-doc she was dating before, but he just moved away, so she's probably looking to replace him," he said with his usual bluntness.

I had been a post-doc myself when she met me and felt somewhat chagrined at the racial connection, but I was so flattered by her interest I hardly cared.

"So she's single?" I asked.

"Sylvia? No, she's got a boyfriend, but she's poly."

"*Poly* - what's that?"

"Polyamorous," Sam said, "it means she dates multiple people at the same time."

It was the first I'd heard of polyamory, and it went against everything I'd known about relationships to that point. "Well that's not for me then," I said, "I'm looking for something serious."

An Apple a Day

"But it's Sylvia!" he said, laughing.

"Whatever," I responded.

I knew what he was getting at. While most of the women I was drawn to were of unconventional appeal, Sylvia was a beauty through every heteronormative lens, with long brown hair, toned slender limbs, classical features, and olive skin. Pretty much every man (and many women) I knew in that circle was interested in her, though she didn't seem to be particularly interested in any of them. I was certainly flattered that a woman who commanded such a high degree of attention would be interested in a strange creature like me, but given her non-single status I tried as best I could to put her out of my mind.

The next time I saw her would be at a summer warehouse party in South Seattle. It was there that I met Corey, the woman who would become my first Seattle girlfriend. Sylvia was flirting with me shamelessly, to the point of coming up to me and stroking my hair while I was talking with Corey. At that point I was more annoyed than flattered, and asked her to leave me alone so I could talk with Corey.

"Fine, fine," she said, raising her hands in a sarcastic gesture of surrender and walking away.

Six months later, I had broken up with Corey. After seeing Sylvia again at a party, I gave in to her delightful charms and we started chatting regularly at parties. We even went on a couple of friendly dates where we talked and laughed together but didn't so much as hold hands. We would have dinner, sometimes coffee, and then go our separate ways. Though she rarely mentioned her boyfriend, I knew he was in the background, and as a result I kept my distance. Despite my best efforts, though, I was feeling more and more drawn to her.

Around this time, I went to a "make-out" party at a friend's house that was notorious for its risqué events. It was a bit outside my comfort zone, but I felt the need to push myself so I could meet someone new and take my mind off Sylvia. After getting a drink to calm my nerves, I started to talk with some new people in the kitchen. Somehow I caught the attention of a lovely young nurse who started talking and flirting with me, but before I knew what was happening, Sylvia cut in between us and kissed me in a long, passionate embrace, pressing her small body against mine. I could overhear the nurse saying, "That's not fair, I didn't even get to kiss him yet," which also surprised and delighted me, but in that moment Sylvia's kiss blocked out all of my other senses; there was me and there was Sylvia and there was nothing else.

"Want to come downstairs with me?" she said with a seductive smile. My head still spinning, I nodded yes.

She led me by the hand to the basement, brought me to an armchair, and pushed me down onto it. She straddled me with her crotch in direct contact with mine. She continued to kiss me, moving her body up and down against me. As she felt the lump growing in my pants but constrained by my clothing she got up for a moment, laughing.

"I'll give you a moment to *adjust* yourself so you're more comfortable," she said with a giggle.

She got back on and continued to kiss me; I could hear vague echoes of people commenting on what we were doing but I was lost to the world. Suddenly when she looked off to the side I realized there was someone else standing next to us: it was her boyfriend, Ishaq. As always, I had hoped against hope that perhaps she had finally broken up with him, but quickly realized this wasn't the case.

"Ishaq, feel how soft his lips are, they're just like a woman's! Su, is it ok if Ishaq kisses you?" she said breathlessly.

I wasn't the slightest bit interested in kissing Ishaq, but at this point I would do anything Sylvia asked, and agreed. It was the first time I had kissed a man, and while I was open to the possibility that such a thing might excite me, kissing Sylvia's boyfriend was of not the kind of first experience I had in mind.

"Mmmmm" he said theatrically, "his lips *are* really soft. Mind if I borrow Sylvia for a bit?" he asked, more a command than a question.

I nodded, and they went around the corner for a few minutes while I sat on the armchair, dazed and overwhelmed by the intensity I'd felt with Sylvia. She came back in a few moments and straddled me again, and I reached up to kiss her she put a hand on my chest and held me back.

"Hey, do you want to come back to our house with Ishaq and me where we could continue this? It's okay if you say no," she said, then released her hand and kissed me again.

"Um, sure..." I said, not happy about having to share her with Ishaq, but far too excited to be with her to refuse.

"Wonderful! You haven't been to our house before?"

"No..." I said, still wondering if I was making the right call.

"No problem. I'll go with you in your car and we'll meet Ishaq there."

We drove to their house on the other side of town; it would be the first of many times I'd navigate the winding roads of their exclusive neighborhood. We walked inside and went straight to their bedroom; Ishaq was already there.

Sylvia wanted to watch Ishaq and I make out but neither of us were very interested; we kissed briefly and he stroked my cock half-heartedly for a few minutes. Soon both of our attention turned to Sylvia – she rubbed her naked body against mine as I lay back in their king-sized bed, while Ishaq tongued her anus from behind. Her face was full of bliss, and she kissed me forcefully while her body heaved against mine.

At some point Ishaq wanted to have sex with her by himself. He waved his hand dismissively towards the other side of their gigantic bed and said, "Why don't you just take care of yourself over there." I awkwardly lay next to them while they moved against each other, Ishaq thrusting into her rapidly until he came. They both made the theatrical-sounding "mmmmm" sound I'd heard from Ishaq at the party, after which Ishaq fell asleep almost immediately.

Once he was clearly unconscious, she turned and whispered into my ear, "Are you awake?"

"Yes," I whispered, turning towards her.

"I want to spend some alone time with you," sliding her hand down my chest and ending at my cock, slowly stroking it as she spoke.

"I'd like that very much," I said, kissing her passionately before falling asleep in her arms.

The next few months, whether I was at work, home, or out with friends, I was thinking about Sylvia. She knew that I was new to polyamory and insisted I continue to date other people while we were seeing each other. I tried to follow her guidance, but given how distracted I was with her it was hard to make much progress. Furthermore, the few times something would start to intensify, Sylvia would get jealous and want more and more of my time. When I confronted her about the hypocrisy of this given that she always had Ishaq to go home to, she said, "Well, my seeing Ishaq doesn't prevent me from seeing you, but I know you want to be monogamous so if something really works out for you, then you won't want to see me anymore." On the one hand, she had a point; on the other, it still felt unfair. On the third hand, I was so obsessed with Sylvia it hardly mattered – I would do anything to keep seeing her.

In addition to being the first polyamorous person I'd dated, Sylvia was also the first who would prove to be more kinky than I was. Though I had quickly learned that Seattleites were far more comfortable discussing and displaying their kinks than those in my conservative circles in Boston, Sylvia continued to surprise me. For instance, she would always want to watch me urinate and hold my penis while I did it, but I felt too embarrassed to comply.

"Why not?" she would whine, "There's nothing to be embarrassed about – I'm telling you it turns me on!"

She would constantly ask me about my fantasies and the things that turned me on, and made it clear from talking about her own experiences that she was a sexual omnivore across both kinks and genders. As such, it was easy to talk to her about my love of butt play and the range of toys I used to pleasure myself. Her eyes lit up when I mentioned the toys: "I want to see them!" she said.

Since I now was working at my first real job, I was able to afford much higher quality equipment, and fortunately Seattle was also home to one of the nation's foremost sex-positive sex shops, Toys in Babeland. I now had a range of silicone butt-plugs and dildos, and proudly showed my collection to my excited lover. Sylvia carefully held and examined each one and asked me how I used it, getting more and more excited as we talked. She asked me which was my favorite, and I pointed at a smooth red-and-black silicone dildo, about an inch and a half in diameter, and curved near the tip to put additional pressure on the prostate. She asked how I used it, and I started describing the process when she interrupted me.

"Don't *tell* me. I want to you to *show* me," she said, her eyes wide.

I was a little hesitant, but she insisted and was clearly very turned on, which was turning me on as well. I arranged two pillows on top of each other and put the plug on top of them, lubed myself up, straddling the pillows, and slowly worked the plug into my body. The pillows pushed it up into me, and I showed her how I would rock back and forth, feeling the smooth silicone bump push up against my g-spot. By this time I had an intense erection and was stroking it with my lubed hand; I had closed my eyes with the intensity of the feeling.

When I opened them, I was surprised to see Sylvia completely naked and mounting me.

"Shouldn't we get a condom?" I asked with alarm.

"It's fine, just don't you *dare* cum inside me, I'm not on any birth control right now."

With that, she lowered herself slowly onto my cock and stared directly in my eyes as we rocked back and forth. It felt incredible, but despite both of us (and Ishaq) having been tested recently, I kept thinking back to the accident with Stella, and after a few thrusts into her body I lifted her off my penis.

"Oh you're no fun," she pouted playfully, but watched eagerly as I brought myself to orgasm.

Because of Sylvia's wide-eyed enthusiasm, I felt much less inhibited about expressing myself. We would talk extensively about what turned us on, I would touch her and let her touch me in ways I hadn't with others, and even kissed her differently, finally feeling comfortable stepping out of the expectations of a traditional male lover and just fusing my body with hers in the ways that felt most natural.

One night after a particularly intense session of kissing she pulled her head back to say, "you know what's strange – you make love like a *woman*, it's really remarkable!"

An Apple a Day

She said it with admiration, and as she often spoke about how she preferred her female lovers to her men, I was beaming. Though it was not something I had sought out, I felt that it was the greatest compliment on my sexuality I had ever received.

I rushed to tell my friend Sam the next day, brimming with excitement; he made a face and said "you probably shouldn't go around repeating that." Suddenly, in the light of traditional masculinity, my greatest compliment had become a mark of shame. Once again, the old words from Mark and Amos echoed through my mind: *nobody wants to see that.*

All of those experiences and moments from the past few months played through my head as she picked me up on the bridge that morning. As she drove towards her neighborhood, she said "I have a surprise for you."

With Sylvia, I had no idea what this would mean, but was already getting turned on. We walked into her empty house and up to her bedroom; she asked me to take all my clothes off, lie back on the bed, and close my eyes. I did as she asked, and after waiting for what seemed like a long time, asked "Can I open them yet?"

"Not yet," she giggled, as she seemed to be struggling with something. "Okay, now you can look."

She had talked about her strap-on before, but this was my first time seeing it up close. It was a cloth-based device built into a pair of thong underwear, with what seemed like a disappointingly small white dildo attached. Still, the thrill of seeing her beautiful body, completely naked but with an erect cock, was turning me on in a way I had never felt before. I spread my legs apart as she carefully lubed up my bottom, then ever so gently started guiding the tip into me. She had a huge smile on her face and her eyes were wide in a way I knew meant that she was extremely turned on. She started moving the tip in and out of me and she looked into my eyes, her mouth open in a wide smile.

I had dreamed of this moment from the moment she had first told me she wanted to fuck me in this way, but the reality was not living up to my expectations. While I was excited to be penetrated for the first time, I had imagined she would be thrusting into me with the full force of her lithe body; instead she was mostly passive, and I wanted more. I grabbed her hips and pulled myself up towards her, my hips in the air and the full dildo inside me, my bare skin pressed up against her pelvis. Her eyes opened wider, and we rocked back and forth like that. She lubed up my cock with her hand and brought me to an explosive orgasm. We both collapsed onto the bed from the intensity of the experience.

"Wow," she said, after catching her breath, "You took that like a pro – I've never had someone pull the whole thing inside themselves!"

An Apple a Day

I laughed and said, "Well, I've had a lot of experience."

We cleaned up, put our clothes back on, and went downstairs to the kitchen. There was a bowl of fruit there and she handed an apple to me. "Well, Dr. Su, I feel like I should give you something for letting me fuck you like that. How about an apple?"

"Sure," I smiled.

"An apple a day keeps the doctor away – or brings the doctor here, I guess, huh?" We both laughed, still high from the experience.

She offered to drive me back to where she picked me up so I could catch my bus to work, and in a few moments I was back to where she had called out to me an hour ago. As I waited for the bus, I ate the apple, hardly believing what had just happened. I had been penetrated by another person for the first time, and not only that, by a woman I was incredibly attracted to. There was still the nagging thought in my brain that it couldn't be just the two of us as I wanted, but for the moment life felt pretty incredible.

In the months that followed, we would never repeat the experience – I got the sense she was more excited by the novelty of it than the experience itself, and I didn't push her on this; I was just happy to be spending time with her. That too became far more complicated as she began to hint that she might leave

Ishaq to be with me, which made me ever more desperate to turn this into a reality. However, after months of discussions, tears, and passionate nights together, one awful night she called me to tell me he asked her to marry him and she had agreed.

While to me it seemed the world was ending, she didn't see why I couldn't just stay with her and continue things as they were. Until that point, I had become completely drawn into the fantasy that we might be together despite how improbable it was, but this woke me up to the reality that she would never leave him. All of a sudden, the situation no longer felt acceptable to me. While I hungered for her, it was tearing me apart to both feel so intensely for her and to know there was no possibility of her ever leaving Ishaq.

Fighting every obsessed fiber of my being, I told her I couldn't date her anymore. In our final conversation as lovers, as I was explaining my reasoning and how I couldn't be with her because she would never be exclusive with me, she put in a final shot.

"Well," she said, "You know the things I did to you? You're not going to find many women who are willing to do that."

I knew exactly what she was talking about, and I was terrified she was right, but still, I knew that continuing in this fantasy would only bring me misery. I stuck to my guns and we ended our sexual relationship that day. I was fairly certain at the time that I would never be penetrated by a woman again, but perhaps it was the price I had to pay to be in a "normal" relationship. Within a week she started dating someone new – a much more masculine man, more like Ishaq than me. I was even there when she met him, and she called me that evening to talk to me about it.

"Did you meet this tall guy, Abir, at the party?" she asked.

"Yes, I think so," I said, tentatively; it would have been hard not to notice them flirting with each other.

"Well, he asked me out, and I think I'm going to say yes," she continued.

I could taste stomach acid in my mouth; I wanted to hang up right then. "Why are you telling me this?" I managed to ask.

"I just wanted to see how you felt about it," she said innocently.

"Well, I feel crappy, how would you think I'd feel," I said, "But you should do whatever makes you happy."

"Don't you get snippy with *me*," she hissed. "Remember, you're the one who wanted to break up with me."

"I know, I know," I said, desolate at how things were turning out. This is not what I had wanted at all.

In attempting to maintain a friendship with her, I agreed to go to a group dinner where she was introducing Abir to our mutual friends. I was miserable enough for most of the dinner seeing them happily holding hands and caressing each other, but the low point was yet to come. Our mutual friend Sam, in a moment of levity, brought up a silly song I'd made up about butt plugs that I never should have shared with him.

"How does it go again, *'I like to put it in my butt... it's like a great big you know what...'*" he asked, half-singing and getting the tune all wrong.

"Yeah, I'd rather not," I said, annoyed and already embarrassed.

"C'mon, Su, we want to hear it!" Sylvia said.

It was always hard for me to say no to her, and against my better judgment, I sang the ridiculous song. The table erupted in laughter, probably mostly with me, but it felt like it was at me. Seeing her and her new lover laughing over something that had been private, beautiful, and sexy between us made me want to sink through the floor. It was as if all of that vulnerable intimacy had been turned into a joke; if not something to be ashamed of, at best something to be ridiculed. I left that dinner resolving not to spend any more time with her, and for the most part managed to hold myself to that.

Within a month, the impossible happened: she finally broke up with Ishaq. I couldn't stop kicking myself – if only I'd held on, perhaps that could have been me instead of Abir. In retrospect, I think it's highly unlikely, and ultimately she didn't stay with this new lover either. So many things about Sylvia felt unreal, it's hard to even imagine what might have been had things gone differently.

To this day, I still walk the Montlake bridge fairly often on my way to work or to the University of Washington, and listen carefully for voices beneath the white noise of the highway below. There are days when I am certain I can hear a voice calling me in the wind, and feel a faint craving for a taste of apple.

A Boy Named Su

Boys Can Be a Real Drag

"*DRAG BALL!*" the flier announced, in hand-drawn capital letters. "*Come one, come all; have a drink, have a ball!*"

I had looked at this flier at least a dozen times since I received it at a party the previous weekend. I laughed to myself every time, as it made me think of the "have a ball" comment I often made with respect to my single testicle, but there was more to it than that. I was interested, even excited, but still unsure if I was ready for another drag party.

I was leaning towards going: it was the only interesting event going on that weekend, and besides, it had been almost a decade since my last drag party. A great deal had also changed since then: Seattle seemed to be a far more accepting city on issues of gender and sexuality, and my experiences with Stella and Sylvia made me more confident about my identity than I had been in the past. Despite the shaming experience I'd had the last time with Mark and Amos, I decided it was worth another try. I had also gained something of a reputation as a costume maker, so I felt I couldn't let down my friends' expectations.

I no longer had the slinky black dress I'd worn in Cambridge, but I had a few days to prepare, and started off by fashioning a skirt from an old t-shirt with my trusty 1967 Singer sewing machine. I picked up a lacy black padded bra from Goodwill and some cheap makeup from the corner drugstore. Once I had all the parts, I pulled a tank top over the bra and put a close-fitting hoodie over the whole thing, the zipper pulled suggestively down to the clasp of the bra. I put on a long-haired black wig I'd used for a different costume, and went to the bathroom to put on the red Wet-n-Wild lipstick I'd picked up from the drugstore. To my surprise, when I looked in the mirror, I didn't feel the immediate dysphoria I had back in Cambridge – perhaps because I already knew I wouldn't look quite as I imagined myself in my mind's eye. Given my lowered expectations, I was surprised at how passable I looked. I played with my hair, added some eye makeup, and soon had a look I felt reasonably pleased with.

The party was in Pioneer Square, a twenty-minute walk from my apartment, and I had planned to take off my wig and bra, put on a long coat, and reassemble the costume upon reaching the venue, just as I had back in Cambridge. The spring night was unexpectedly warm, though, and given how accepting Seattle seemed to be and how early it was in the evening, I didn't see the harm in just walking there in costume. More importantly, I'd spent so much time on perfecting my look at this point, I didn't want to have to reconstruct it in some dark club bathroom. I zipped up my hoodie to a more modest setting, stuffed some "male" clothes into a backpack, and headed out into the night.

The first few moments felt exhilarating; I had never been out in public in a female skin, and though nobody was paying any attention to me, somehow the entire world felt different. I walked to the next block and noticed three men walking towards me, white "frat boy" types in t-shirts and backwards baseball caps. I ran into these types all the time in my downtown neighborhood; I ignored them and they ignored me, so I thought nothing of it. Tonight, unfortunately, would prove to be very different.

By the time we were within half a block of each other, the men started hooting and hollering towards me. I didn't really know what to make of it; they were clearly drunk, and I certainly didn't want to interact with them. I considered crossing to the other side of the street, but thought that might just draw more attention; instead I put my head down and started walking faster.

The man in the middle was more aggressive than his friends, and kept calling out to me the closer we came, "Hey baby, c'mon, what's up, let's see a smile, c'mon!"

My heart had begun to beat faster; I was genuinely nervous at this point, and I kept my head down and continued walking as fast as I could.

As we crossed each other on the sidewalk walked I heard one of the boys cry out, "Oh SHIIIIT! It's a DUDE!"

Suddenly the middle boy went from plying catcalls to venomous rage.

"What the FUCK," he yelled, "I'm gonna MESS YOU UP, DUDE."

At this point I was walking away as fast as I could, hoping they were too drunk to keep up with me. I took a quick look over my shoulder, and saw the middle man being held back by his friends, his face contorted with anger, his neck straining. I could faintly hear his companions saying, "it's not worth it, man, c'mon, just let it go." I didn't look back again.

I was terrified. As much as I wanted to give up on the evening and crawl back into my bed, at this point it was too late to head back home, as that would lead me back towards these men. Even the thought of hailing a cab in costume filled me with even more dread, not wanting to trust anyone at this point. Instead, I kept my head down and walked as fast as I could to the party. Not a single other person gave me a second glance the rest of the way, but my heart was still racing with the shock of what I had just experienced. I walked into the party on high alert, and only calmed down after seeing a friend at the door and getting my first drink.

To my surprise, the event was sparsely attended, and I knew almost nobody there; apparently my usual crowd had ended up somewhere else. Somewhat relieved at not having to talk about what happened, I went to the mostly empty dance floor as I felt that dancing would help me calm down. The DJ was excellent, and after a few songs I was finding my groove and had mostly put the experience of the walk out of my mind.

After a while, I noticed a woman with a costume moustache and a comically large dildo attached to her small frame who kept turning to look at me as she danced. I moved closer to her and she gave me a friendly smile; we started dancing with each other, and before long she was rubbing her dildo up between my legs as she held my waist and I held her shoulders. I wasn't really sure if she was drawn to me because of my costume, because of the boy behind the costume, or if she just wanted someone to dance with, but I was feeling increasingly turned on. As she pulled her dildo against my crotch, she felt under my skirt – as she felt the hardness there, she gave me a big grin and kissed me.

We had been dancing like that for an hour or more, her dildo pushing my skirt up between my legs, when she got a call on her phone.

"Oh, it's work, it looks like I have to head out," she said.

"Oh," I said, disappointed that the experience was coming to an end. "Do you want to maybe, um, hang out sometime?" I asked awkwardly.

"Sure," she smiled, and handed me her card, which felt like an oddly formal gesture. Seeing my expression, she explained, "That's actually my cellphone number; I own my own business."

"Ah, got it," I replied brightly. "Actually, I think I'm going to take off too," I said, excited by our connection but also ready to put this night behind me.

I went into the bathroom, pulled the familiar male clothes out of my backpack, stuffed my female costume inside, and wiped off most of the makeup. I walked back out onto the dance floor, and to my surprise, she was still there.

"Woah," she said, eyes widening, "you clean up nicely!" and walked over to kiss me again.

I had mixed feelings about this comment: on the one hand, I was glad she found my masculine form attractive, but on the other, I had felt *seen* in my feminine form, and had been drawn to her from that perspective. Now recasting myself into my male identity, I was uncertain about my attraction to her, and as we hugged and kissed goodbye I wasn't sure whether I wanted to call her back.

I left the venue and walked towards home, no longer terrified, since I was back in the safety of my male costume. At this time, things were still at their peak with Sylvia, and given our busy schedules we'd often call each other late in the evening to see if we could find a few hours to be together. Halfway home my phone rang and I saw it was her.

"Are you doing anything tonight?" she asked.

"I'm just heading home from a party now; it was quite an experience," I said, thinking back to the harrowing experience earlier in the evening.

"What happened?" she said, concerned, hearing the edge in my voice. "Can I come over?" she asked.

"Sure, just come over," I said, looking forward to seeing her and being able to talk about what happened.

By the time I reached my building she was already at the door; once we were safely inside I told the whole story to her, the way the men had acted, the terror I felt when their catcalls turned into the threat of violence.

"Oh Su!" she said, "You should have known better than to go out in the street like that."

"But that's just it," I protested, "I was just wearing a hoodie and a skirt. And regardless, shouldn't a woman be able to walk down the street without being harassed or threatened?"

She sighed, "Welcome to what it's like to be a woman *—every single day.*"

That made me pause; indeed, I hadn't thought about how fortunate I was to be able to take off the costume and return to the safety of my maleness, how different the walk home was from the walk to the party. She wanted to see my costume and asked me to recreate it for her, but I had been through too much that night to redo the makeup or recapture the confidence I had felt. All I wanted was to hold her warm body close to me and go to sleep, and she was happy to comply.

In the years since, I've told this story many times to illustrate a moment when I gained insight into the danger women face on the streets every day, as well as the privilege of safety that men have purely by virtue of their maleness. It was only recently, though, that a female friend responded to my story with, "Well sure, I've felt fear with some catcallers, but I've never experienced what it would feel like as a transwoman who incurred the wrath of homophobic men."

I've thought about that comment quite a bit since then. I can't help but think of Islan Nettles, whose story began so similarly to mine: she was killed in Brooklyn in 2013 by a man who was initially attracted to her but then erupted in angry violence when he realized she was a transwoman. She's far from the only one, though: so many others have been killed or severely injured at the hands of men, for nothing more than the crime of breaking gender stereotypes. The anger of these men at their own attraction was so great they felt there was no other recourse than to injure or even kill the person who had created those feelings. There's even a legal term used to justify this kind of twisted violence – "gay panic" or "trans panic." Sadly, many states in the US still allow this as a valid defense for assault and even murder.

I feel fortunate that I survived that night and did not end up as a statistic; at the same time, it forever changed me, both giving me more insight into the lived experience of women and also making me startlingly aware of the risks of expressing the full spectrum of my gender. Though I had started to overcome my feelings of shame around my gender, I was only beginning to understand the real dangers of being who I was.

A Boy Named Su

But I'm Asking You To

In my first few years in Seattle, I still woke up and went to bed on a grad student schedule. It was hard to get out of bed, let alone out of the house and into the office, at the unreasonable hour of 9am. My group had a "midmorning" daily meeting at 10:30, so this meant at the latest catching the 9:58 bus, which meant getting out of bed by 8:30 (horrors!). Most days I would be running just to make it, and as luck would have it, the last stretch to the bus stop was uphill.

This was the fall after breaking up with Sylvia, during a long period of singlehood, so I didn't even have the excuse of a night of passion wearing me out – I just didn't like getting up early. As I huffed and puffed my way to my stop day after day, I started to notice a lovely woman running down the hill in a blue checkered coat at the same time. We began to recognize each other, flashing a quick smile on the sidewalk as we hurried along to our respective destinations. I desperately wanted to meet her, but felt that it would be much too forward to stop and talk to her. I agonized over how I might reach out, and eventually decided I would write her a note. It started off as a simple hello and a phone number, but as I worked through and crumpled draft after draft, it turned into three elaborate stanzas of rhyming verse:

> *In checkered blue you hurry by,*
> *Down Olive Street, past 8th, where I*
> *Am waiting for the bus I ride*
> *To work:*
>
> *And shyly with my quiet eye*
> *I catch your glance and tiny smile*
> *At two 'til ten, the bus comes by:*
> *I board—*
>
> *And though we go our sep'rate ways,*
> *Your smile stays with me all the day,*
> *And so I'll take this risk to say:*
> *Hello.*

I added my name and email, folded it up into my pocket, and headed out as usual on a late November morning, determined to hand it to her. I ran up the last leg to the bus stop, saw her coming down the hill, took a deep breath, and walked right up to my commuter crush.

As I did, I reached in my pocket, and found – nothing. My smile quickly faded, and she turned to look at me quizzically, smiling; all I could do was smile back. Had I left the note at home? Had I lost it along the way? How could this have happened?

Fortunately, I'd kept the original draft of the poem in a journal, so I was able to reconstruct it at home. The next day I came prepared – I had written out two different copies and put them in two different pockets; I would not be thwarted so easily. When I arrived at the bus stop, though, she didn't show up at all that day; nor the next day, nor the day after that. Crestfallen, I continued to carry the notes in my pockets, but wondered if my opportunity had passed for good.

To my relief, she reappeared a week later, just as suddenly as she had disappeared, and this time I was ready. I handed her the note – she looked surprised but said a quiet "thank you" and continued running down the hill.

She wrote to me the very next day, a sweet hello thanking me for reaching out and expressing an interest in seeing me again. Our first few dates were innocent and friendly: digging through used CDs, a cup of coffee on Broadway, a steaming bowl of Pho. The more I got to know her, the more I liked her, and I wanted to spend more intimate time with her; cautiously, I invited her over to watch my favorite movie, *Amelie,* on a Saturday night.

"Oh!" she said, "That sounds lovely, but I can't Saturday, since I'm going to this end-of-the-year battle-of-the-bands event at the Mars Bar! Do you want to come with me?"

"Sure..." I said hesitantly, less sure of myself in a crowded setting with unfamiliar music, and expecting she'd want to bring other friends along.

"Well, maybe we could do both!" she returned, and I smiled to myself, as that could still mean a late night at my place, and a chance for us to finally be alone together.

I picked her up at her place, and I learned that her original plan was to have gone alone, so it would just be the two of us after all. The show was fun; she knew many more of the bands than I did, but she stayed by my side the whole night, even when dancing. By the end she was standing in front of me and holding my hands to pull me against her, at which point I didn't really care what music was playing. When we left the show she took me to a hidden parking lot with a breathtaking view of Lake Union; I readied myself for our first kiss, but she turned it into a hug and said, "C'mon, we'd better get that movie started!"

But I'm Asking You To

We went back to my place and started the movie. I had hoped we would cuddle up in each other's arms, but she wanted to sit on the floor in front of the couch, so I sat somewhat awkwardly behind her. She leaned up against my legs and I occasionally put my hand on her shoulder and she would reach up to play with my fingers, but the feeling was not particularly intimate. I was at least beginning to feel more comfortable being close to her, and felt that while things were not going to go any further that night, I was happy with how it had turned out – we had spent a pleasant evening and had some good alone time together; physical intimacy would come soon enough.

Before the movie was even finished, though, she surprised me by asking if we could go to the bedroom. A little nervous but excited by her interest, I agreed, and we quickly pulled off each other's clothes. She lay back on the bed and pulled me close to her. I grabbed a condom, but as I opened it, I felt my erection rapidly disappear.

I went pale: this had never happened before. I desperately pulled at my penis to no avail. She looked up to see what was wrong, and tried to stimulate me, but nothing was working. I was getting more and more anxious and embarrassed, and though she was trying to calm me and assure me it was okay, I felt miserable. Eventually we gave up and went to sleep together. I drove her home the next morning, hugged her goodbye, and expected to never hear from her again. I was ready to put this embarrassing experience behind me – clearly it was just not meant to be.

A week later I was at a conference in Canada, and she surprised me again, this time with a sweet email. She said she really enjoyed the time we spent together, that she missed me, and that she was wondering when we could see each other again. She apologized for *her* awkwardness, which I could hardly understand given what had happened. I was completely floored – I had been certain she would never give me another chance. She also told me that she was about to leave town for Christmas, so we decided on an evening in early January to see each other again.

This time we met for dinner and had more time to spend together at my place, slowly warming each other up and getting to know each other's bodies. By the time we were ready to have sex I had a strong erection but was beginning to feel nervous again, and as I reached my arm out for a condom she stopped me and shook her head. I reached for it again and she grabbed my hand and shook her head again. I looked at her, not certain what she meant, and she gently cradled my penis in her hands, making my erection even stronger than it already was. She started rubbing the tip against her vulva, letting me feel the wetness. We had both been tested recently, but there was still the very real risk of pregnancy, and I hesitated. I started to say something, and she put her left hand to my lips, and with her right gently guided the head of my penis inside her.

She felt wet and warm and wonderful; my whole body lit up with the feeling of her holding me inside her. Conscious of the dangers we were toying with, I was going to pull myself out after a few slow strokes, but she held on to me and pulled me back in. After feeling myself get close I did pull out and she slowly stroked me to completion in an intense and shuddering orgasm.

"Now wasn't that nice?" she smiled at me.

"It was incredible," I said.

The next few months passed like a dream. I had never felt such intense chemistry with someone – as soon as she would open the door, smiling up at me, and I held her against my body, breathing in her intoxicating scent: I wanted her, and she wanted me. She had a formidable intellect and we enjoyed talking to each other as well, but we would often end up in bitter arguments over seemingly small things, like the under-lying meaning of a classic novel or the relative merits of lovers spending a day in complete silence with each other. No matter how much we would fight, though, we would always ending up having sex, and couldn't get enough of each others' bodies.

A Boy Named Su

One night when we had become much more comfortable with each other sexually, she got on her knees on the bed with her face in the pillow and asked me to spank her. I was horrified.

"No, I can't do that!" I said; feeling dark echoes of distant memories from childhood.

"Why not?" she asked.

"Because it's bad," I said, aware that I sounded like a five-year old, "you shouldn't hit other people."

"But I'm *asking you to!*" she said, frustrated.

"No, I can't, I just can't." I said, collapsing onto the bed.

She could see I was upset and let it go. It was unlike her, though, to let anything go for long. The next night we were together, she had a proposal.

"What if I do it to you, and you can see what it's like?"

"Well, okay," I reluctantly agreed, not particularly thrilled about this, but knew she wouldn't intentionally hurt me.

I got down in the same position she had been in, head buried in the pillow, bottom up in the air. She started stroking my bottom, running her hands all over the surface, gently running her fingers in the groove between and stroking my penis. Without warning, she then gave a sharp slap to one cheek. To my surprise, not only was it not unpleasant, it was really turning me on. I felt my back starting to arch back and forth and my bottom sway slightly from side to side; I wanted more.

It felt wonderful to be under her power, oddly reminiscent of the fantasy I'd had about firm hands caressing me back in Cambridge. At that time, I had believed only male hands could play that role, but this was a much sexier reality I had never even considered. She continued to alternate soft caresses and sharp slaps, caresses and slaps, and I was absolutely loving it.

"Well I can tell from the amount of precum that you don't think this is so bad," she giggled.

"You're right," I said, my voice muffled by the pillow, "this is very different from what I had imagined."

Once she had shown me how pleasurable it could be, I was ready to try it on her. I took her same approach, alternating soft touch with slaps, and saw her getting turned on in much the same ways I'd felt my body reacting – her back arching up and down, her bottom moving, her vulva becoming increasingly wet. After fifteen minutes of slow spanking she called out in a ragged voice, "could you please fuck me, *hard*?" I pushed her down onto the bed, and as I was extremely turned on as well was only able to enter her for a short time before having to pull out, knowing I would come soon.

"Why did you stop?" she asked, turning her head around.

"I was about to come," I said, breathing heavily.

"You're not going to get me pregnant, silly," she giggled.

I looked at her skeptically. Perhaps she knew her cycle well enough that this was true, but it wasn't a risk I was willing to take.

After the spanking episode, we opened up to each other sexually to a far greater degree. She had noticed how much I enjoyed having my bottom stimulated, and on a sunny afternoon in February she asked me how I would feel about penetrated. I told her it was one of my favorite things – I saw a smile spread across her face, and in a moment we had left her place and were out shopping for strap-ons.

We walked the two blocks over to Toys in Babeland, where a helpful attendant told us the pros and cons of different harnesses while we held hands and listened intently, both very excited about what was coming next. I had several dildos I liked at home, so we just picked a harness – a high-end Western-themed affair hand crafted from high-quality leather, with a buckle at the waist as well as one on each leg for an optimal fit and a metal O-ring on which to mount the dildo. The attendant was delighted to see us so happy with our purchase. He put it into one of their bright pink (and impossible to miss) bags, and we were on our way. We were less than a block out of the store when we ran into my friend Sam, who I had not seen much of since that last. disastrous dinner with Sylvia.

"Hey, you two," he said, "what did you get from Babeland?" pointing to the bag.

"Oh, nothing," we giggled, at this point no longer able to contain our excitement.

"Nothing?" he smiled.

"Yeah, um, nothing. Well, we've got to go!" I said, and we ran off laughing, hand in hand.

We had talked about where we would try it for the first time and we decided to use my place, as I had both the dildo and the lube that would work best for my bottom. We drove straight there, spending fifteen confused minutes figuring out how to put on and tighten the complex harness for the first time, and then were finally ready to go. In my fantasies I was most excited about lying face down on the bed, my legs slightly parted, so I got into this position. She lubed me up very carefully, and slowly started to enter me. As it always took me a little while to take in the larger dildo, I helped her provide gentle, repeated pressure until I could take it in.

Before long, the whole dildo was inside me, and I expected her to start thrusting herself in and out of my body like in my fantasies. Instead, she very gingerly pushed forward, then carefully back, peeking around to see my face.

"Can you go harder?" I asked, frustrated.

"I just don't want to hurt you," she said.

"It's fine, don't worry," I said, but she kept worriedly looking at my face.

"I want to see your face," she said.

"Why," I asked, frustrated at getting distracted from the experience.

"I want to see how it's feeling for you," she replied.

I wasn't really prepared for this, and just wanted her to drive hard into me without thinking about me. I hadn't thought at all about how *she* might feel about that. Though initially frustrated by her timidity, I began to understand how this was a much more complex dynamic than my fantasy, one we would both have to learn to navigate with each other.

After that night we would alternate almost every time; one night I would fuck her, the next she would fuck me. We got better at our communication, and while she would never drive into me with quite the level of dominance I desired, I loved the feeling of having her inside of me. After one particularly intense session, we were laying in bed together and she was absent-mindedly stroking my chest.

"You know," she said, "I don't think I want to date any more guys that won't let me do that."

"But you said I'm the first person you've done this with!" I said, incredulously.

"Yes, and I love it!"

"So do you think all the guys you date will be OK with this?"

"Well they better be, or they can't date me!" she said, pouting.

I greatly admired her confidence, and wished I felt sure enough of myself to apply the same standard to my own future lovers, but this was something I still felt a great deal of shame about. For instance, despite my deep level of comfort with her, I had not been able to ask for it directly; it was her leading the way and sensing my needs that got us there at all.

Despite the intensity of our desire for each other, our fights continued to grow longer and more frequent, and eventually we broke off our formal relationship. Within a few weeks, though, the hunger for each other grew too strong, and we got together again for sex, telling each other it would be the last time. Then it happened again, and again, and again, until it was almost every weekend. We told each other we weren't dating, and indeed we would both go out with other people, but we would still end up in each other's arms almost every weekend.

It was the following December before I really began to appreciate how perfect our chemistry was for each other, how immediately we could turn each other on despite our awkward beginnings or our constant fights. Before the end of the year, though, she had started seeing someone at work who would rapidly become a serious and exclusive relationship. On December 30th we spent the night together, watching the old Franklin and Bass stop-motion classic, *Rudolph the Red-Nosed Reindeer*. We cuddled up naked under a blanket, forgoing sex to just be close to each other as that cold, clear night turned into the last day of the year.

Though I didn't know it then, it would be the last time we would be intimate with each other. While we would occasionally chat or see each other for dinner in the months before she moved in with her new boyfriend, the closeness we had could be no more. For years afterwards I kicked myself for not recognizing how rare that connection was, though I would always remind myself of the intensity of our fights as well. I do not know what would have happened had we stayed together, but I am always grateful to her for loving and nurturing a submissive part of me that had waited for so long to be seen.

Only When I'm Dancing

When I think of truly masterful flirting, I think of Sylvia. Though she didn't use her powers often, the few times she did, the effects were remarkable (when they were directed at me) and devastating (when they were directed elsewhere). Without being creepy, overly forward, presumptuous, or awkward, she would make her interest clear while maintaining a friendly innocence.

For example, long before the night when she slipped in front of another woman to kiss me for the first time, we ran into each other at a different party. We got into an involved discussion of whether the vast number of new news sources available via the internet would lead to people being better informed or just falling deeper into their own echo chambers. It was a topic both of us had a lot of interest in, and we were enjoying the opportunity to really get into it. At one point, she said, "My hope is that our children..." and then stopped midsentence to turn her head and look directly in my eyes, "well, not *our* children," and then with the briefest of pauses, "well, *maybe* our children," giggling and shyly looking away as she finished her thought.

We both laughed, but months later I noticed how I had remembered that moment, how that pause, phrase, and gesture had burned into my memory, and was one of the first times I was fully aware of her interest in me. She signaled to me, I noticed her signal, and I would never think of her the same way again. Our first date occurred less than a week afterwards. In later months, when we had parted ways and she started pursuing someone else, I saw those skills from a different perspective, a part of me wishing that they were still directed at me.

I, on the other hand, am on the opposite end of the flirting spectrum. My attempts are always awkward, because as soon as I shyly approach someone I'm interested in, I begin obsessing about how being overtly flirtatious could be unwelcome or even frightening, and resort to taking on a very friendly demeanor that is clearly non-threatening. The more interested I am in someone, the more self-conscious I become, and thus the less likely they are to be able to recognize my flirtation. It's effective in that I have no trouble meeting people, since those I approach trust the sincerity of my friendliness, but they rarely have any inkling that I am attracted to them or have a romantic interest.

Only When I'm Dancing

Over the years, I've had many former crushes confide to me that when we first met (usually years before), they had been interested in me and either felt I wasn't interested in them or that I wasn't interested in women at all. Given my approach, style, and genderqueerness, it's never a surprise to me, but it's always disappointing. As much as I've tried, I've never figured out how to get past this. I have no desire to be a manipulative, misogynistic predator like the so-called "pick-up artists" – I simply wish I could innocently express my flirtatious desires the way Sylvia did.

There is an exception, though. Somehow, when I am on the dance floor, everything is different. If the music is right and I am moving with it, I feel so much more comfortable approaching someone, dancing near them, smiling, watching for their reactions, and getting closer if they let me in. Even the type of music hardly matters; whether it's salsa-dancing to a live band or freestyle dancing in a strobe-filled industrial space, I feel an immediate comfort and ease towards those I am attracted to that I never feel while standing next to them at the bar. I feel that I am perceived differently in these situations as well – which can be wonderful in the moment, but sometimes leads to confusion when they interact with me afterwards.

I think there's something about dancing that makes my dance partners feel more connected to me as well. There have been moments on the dance floor that have been deeply surprising to both parties involved. I remember one particular woman who I had known and been attracted to for years without her ever having shown any interest in me. At a mutual friend's wedding, the first time we danced together, after a few turns and spins she pulled closer to me than I would have expected. Resting her head softly on my shoulder, she whispered, "I want to make beautiful brown babies with you."

"Really?" I smiled, flattered but taken aback by the serious tone in which she said it.

"Sort of," she said, turning to look at her husband seated in a chair on the edge of the dance floor. "I never should have married that guy."

Despite my attraction to her, I didn't want to interfere with their marriage (which fell apart soon afterwards), and shied away any from further contact. It struck me, though, that were it not for that moment on the dance floor, our mutual attraction might never have been made clear to either of us.

Another dear soul who I met at a weekly dance event would always seek me out to dance with, sharing touch, expression, and playful laughter with me; it was weeks of this before we ever met off the dance floor. When we did go out, it was not what either of us expected. Sitting together in a sunny café, we were awkward and shy, unable to connect in the way both of us wanted to. Certainly not every dance floor connection translates into the everyday world, but had we met in more ordinary circumstances, we may never have connected at all.

Rejection, also, is far less painful or embarrassing on the dance floor – if I go up to someone and they don't want to dance, they turn away, and I go off to dance somewhere else: no harm, no foul. If we do dance together and feel chemistry on the dance floor, I also feel a great degree of confidence in our physical compatibility. For those lovers with whom I've danced with before becoming intimate, powerful dance floor chemistry has nearly always led to powerful bedroom chemistry.

It is no accident, I think, that the fluidity I feel when dancing feels analogous to the fluidity I feel about my gender. My dancing is neither particularly masculine nor feminine, and both women and men have remarked on the fluid nature of my motions. Just as with physical attraction, I would not expect it to appeal to everybody, but for those to whom it does, it is perhaps a clue towards the fluidity of my spirit. On the dance floor, I feel free of the constraints of a gendered role and can just show up as who I am.

It would be transformative if I could treat every potential flirtation like a dance floor, but I am not there yet. Most days, I stay within my costume, hoping someone might see through it, but not expecting them to. Sometimes, though, when music is right and the lights are low, I take off the costume and ask someone to dance.

The Dragon and the Dominatrix

"Well this is very nice, let's see what's down here," she said, looking directly into my eyes through her mask as she stroked her hand down my chest. To my surprise (and delight), she reached into my underwear and lightly stroked my cock. "And I see this is very nice as well," she said with a smile.

It was the Saturday night of the Seattle Erotic Arts Festival, and while I knew things could get a little wild, I had not expected this to happen in the middle of a crowded dance floor. I found her extremely attractive, and while part of me felt awkward about it happening in such a public space, I was glad that for once, expressing myself with my costume had actually worked out the way I had hoped. I had been gifted a pair of gorgeous silicone rubber dragon wings with a six foot wingspan along with matching dragon claw gloves; I coupled that with fishnet tights, tiny spandex briefs, black lipstick, and crosses of electrical tape over my nipples. My costume idea was to be a "drag-on," i.e., a cross between dressing in drag and a dragon. As I put on the outfit and saw myself in the mirror, I thought I looked sexy and attractive, hoping that the right woman might feel the same – and now it was happening.

"Tell me," she said, stroking soft circles around my nipples, "Do you feel that as a gay man you need to cover your nipples?"

I laughed. "Well, I'm not gay," I said.

She jumped back, visibly alarmed, pulling her hand out of my briefs. "You're not gay?"

"No," I said again, becoming concerned at where this was going.

"You mean you like women?"

"Yes," I said.

"Women like me?" she asked, incredulously, pointing at herself and taking a step back.

"Yes," I said again, thinking perhaps this could still work out.

"Oh, wow," she said, "I never would have touched you like that if I knew you weren't gay," she said.

"It's fine," I said, trying to be flirty, but again feeling the moment slip away.

"Let me introduce you to my friend," she said, scurrying off to find someone who had as little interest in a drag-on as I had in her. All my confidence in my outfit immediately collapsed. What I had thought would be sexy and attractive instead had led a potential match to make all the wrong assumptions. I told the story to a few friends at the party, and more or less everyone said some variant of, "well, what did you expect?" I had expected *to be seen,* but I should have realized this was an unrealistic expectation.

For most of my dating life I have tried to fit into the masculine shell and done what I feel is a reasonable job of it. Compared to other men, perhaps I'm a little too fashionable, with a voice that's perhaps a little too high, but still I can pass as a "regular guy." That is largely the place from which I have tried to attract and flirt with potential partners, hoping that as they get to know me they will discover and love the whole me, not just this outer shell. A few times, it has worked out splendidly; other times, it has ended in disaster.

The most dramatic of these disasters was Heather, a promising partner from the summer after my bus stop romance. Never had I wanted to be more normal than when I met her. Heather was a New Englander, straight out of the J. Crew catalogs of my youth – dimpled smile, curly red hair, a ready smile, and the cable-knit sweaters that so defined my childhood fantasies. Her coffee table had neat stacks of recent J.

Crew catalogs, different from the ones of my youth, but their presence made me feel like fate was calling out to me. This was my chance to play the part of the rugby-playing boyfriend (hopefully without actually having to play rugby), coming in from an afternoon of roughhousing with the boys to snuggle up together on the couch.

She took the same bus as I did to and from work, and we would often sit next to each other, talking and laughing the entire way. In the evenings, I would see her regularly at a neighborhood bar on the way home, and one warm summer night she invited me to join her and her friends. I asked her out dancing with my friends the following week, and despite orders from her doctor to avoid movement due to a recent skin surgery, she joined me on the dance floor. It felt a little bit awkward, but I chalked it up to her recent surgery and being careful with her motions.

A few nights later she called me from a different bar near my place and asked if I wanted to join. I happened to be nearby, just leaving a costume party with some friends. "I'd love to join!" I said. "Would it be ok if I came in costume? I'm just leaving a party!"

She hesitated for a moment, "Well... I'm not sure about how these friends would react..." she began.

"Oh, no problem," I said quickly, "I'll just run home and change first."

"That would be great!" she said with what sounded like relief.

I was caught off guard but didn't think too much of it; perhaps she just didn't want her friends to get the wrong first impression. To my surprise, when I showed up at the bar, it was friends of hers that I already knew, and when I mentioned the party I had just been at, they laughed and said I should have come in costume. Again, I didn't think much of it, but perhaps I should have.

Heather and I absolutely loved talking to each other. Just as we had entertained each other on the bus countless evenings on our hour-long commute, we kept each other talking and laughing over drinks, over dinner, over breakfast, and snuggling together on her couch. Both avid readers and news junkies, we always had things to talk about, and we even shared a common love of stuffed animals and discussed the various adventures they would go on. It was a joy to see her at the end of any day; her smile and warm embrace would warm my heart regardless of my mood.

The bedroom, though, was another matter entirely – our chemistry was just never quite right. I was very attracted to her, and she to me; we would lovingly caress each other for hours on the couch, but once we took off our clothes in the bedroom, everything changed. She always insisted the lights should be turned off, and once every Saturday night (and only Saturday night) wanted to get straight to missionary position without any foreplay. I was happy to accommodate, and I enjoyed the physical sensations, but I would never feel the intensity or connection I had experienced with other lovers.

The one signal I had that she was turned on and excited about lovemaking was her body's response to these sessions: as soon as I would touch her she would feel wonderfully wet, and I would feel confident about her being ready and enthusiastic for sex. Other than this physical indicator, she would be quite still and silent, which I chalked up to her conservative upbringing. One night about six months into our relationship, we started our well-rehearsed lovemaking session as usual, but when I gently caressed her vulva it felt completely dry. I kept stroking the outside and softly drifting a finger inside her, but I couldn't feel a drop of moisture. I gently moved my hand away and pulled up alongside her on the bed.

"Why don't we just cuddle tonight?" I said with a kiss.

"Wait, why did you stop?" she said, sounding surprised.

"We don't have to have sex tonight," I responded, kissing her again, not wanting to go into details.

"But why?" she said, "We always have sex on Saturdays."

"Well…" I said hesitatingly, "I just feel like you're not feeling it tonight."

"What do you mean?" she asked, genuinely confused, "I feel the same as I always do!"

"But," I said, a little surprised myself now, "usually when I touch you down there, you're already wet, but today you're not, so I thought you weren't interested in sex tonight."

"Ohhhhh," she said, laughing. "Well that's easy to explain. I'm only ever wet down there because I put on lube while you're in the bathroom. Tonight you didn't go to the bathroom so I didn't have time."

"Oh!" I said, "you put on lube? I thought you were just excited!"

"Well, it turns out I haven't felt any sexual response for the last ten years," she said matter-of-factly, "ever since I started taking anti-depressants."

"WHAT?" I cried, sitting up in the bed.

"What's the big deal?" she asked, confused.

"You mean all this time we were having sex, you had no interest in it at all?"

"Well it didn't hurt or anything," she replied.

"But still! I thought you were enjoying it!" I was gasping with shock.

"Well it clearly made *you* happy, and it was totally fine with me. Except for oral, I hate oral, it feels all wet and gross."

I was utterly mortified; all this time I had just been pleasuring myself and she had no interest in our lovemaking.

"This is awful," I said, "how could you not tell me?"

"Oh come on," she returned, now feeling self-conscious and annoyed, "I'm sure there are things about you that you haven't told me either."

I paused for a moment, considering. In that moment of vulnerability, I decided it was as good a moment as any to talk about it. "Well, that's true," I said slowly, "I really enjoy having my bottom played with, like with a strap-on."

"WHAT?" she cried; it was her turn to be shocked. "So you want me to dress up like some kind of DOMINATRIX?" she yelled, "when were you going to tell me this?"

"N-no," I stuttered, suddenly embarrassed, "I don't want you dress up like a 'dominatrix,' that's not it at all."

"Well I can't just be a DOMINATRIX, just like that, you know, I've never done anything like that."

"I'm not asking you to, and I don't need you to do anything at all, I'm just saying it's something I like that I haven't told you about," I said, feeling the shame rise up in a hot, familiar wave.

We went on like this for another half hour and somehow managed to get to sleep. We talked it over the cautiously the next morning, both of our guards up, leaving on shaky but amicable terms.

We continued our relationship for another few months, trying different things to create the chemistry we never had, but we had lost a significant amount of trust that night, and we never really recovered. When we finally broke up, she told me she didn't even like dancing, which surprised me.

"But you danced with me that very first night, even when the doctor told you not to!" I said.

"I wanted to be perceived as *fun*," she responded, looking down. "Well I guess it's all for naught now."

We were both disappointed; what had seemed like a perfect relationship was dissolving in front of our eyes.

For years afterwards I painted myself as the victim in this situation – how could Heather have withheld the truth about her sexuality from me? And how dare she compare that to me talking about something I happened to enjoy? It was some years before I could see that in reality we were both doing the same thing – hiding within our costumes. Both of us longed to be accepted, longed to be loved, but neither of us believed we could be loved for who we really were. In fact, we were so certain that we didn't even try; instead we wearily climbed into our 'perfect' costumes, night after night, relationship after relationship, hoping against hope that maybe someday we would find someone with whom we would could take off the costume, lie naked and fully exposed, and somehow, *somehow*, still be loved as we wanted to be.

While this approach protected us in the early stages, ultimately it set us up not only for rejection but also for confirmation of our greatest fears. When our Earthly lovers would finally see us without our costumes, as much as they would try, as much as they would want to still love us, they would turn away in horror and disgust and run screaming from the room. We desperately hoped for something different, but every time we put on the costumes, we were sealing ourselves into the same fate. I wish I could say we learned from the experience, but both of us went on to repeat this pattern again and again for years, hoping that someday, someone might love us enough to peel back the costume and still accept us for who we are.

Don't Lose Your Nerve

I took the post down again. It was the third time that day: there were just too many responses, and most of them were not only failing to turn me on, they were downright scary. I saw threats of violence (intending to be sexy – "I'll tie you up, throw you down on the bed, and then...") when I'd asked for nothing of the sort, ungrammatical half-sentences, commands to "hit the sheets," and countless pictures of penises of every shape and size, soft and erect, tiny and alarmingly large. I was about to delete all of the messages when I ran across the one from Zakai. It was calm, well-written, addressed the specific questions I had raised, and most importantly, it was sane.

The post I'd made was in a discreet corner of the internet known as "casual encounters" on craigslist, eradicated in 2018 by the passage of SESTA/FOSTA. On that forum, one could express their innermost desires and post a photo, then receive responses from those who were interested, with both sides anonymized to each other. After the breakup with Heather and spending many nights thinking about why I kept trying to hide the full spectrum of my sexual desires, I asked myself the question I used to ask so often as a teenager – couldn't all of my challenges with women be explained by a hidden desire for men? My immediate answer was always no, but what if that was just because I had been conditioned by my upbringing and society to think that way? Was I stopping myself from feeling the attraction and desire for what I wanted most?

I went back and forth for weeks – if I really wanted men, why was I always attracted to women, for as long as I could remember? Most of my gay male friends talked about their first crushes being on men, yet I had never felt even a tinge in that direction, while having crushes on literally thousands of women. But what if I was bisexual? Wouldn't it be wonderful to double my potential dating pool? Especially given that men were constantly flirting with me?

The one man I'd been in bed with, Ishaq (with Sylvia), hadn't turned me on at all. And the large man who had pressed his erect cock against my bottom on a very crowded Boston T car had only made me feel violated and angry. But maybe I just wasn't attracted to *those men*, and would be attracted to the *right men*. Furthermore, those were situations I had been pushed into in one form or another, rather than having sought them out. Still, I thought, how could it be that I'd met so many men over my life and never felt drawn to any of them? These questions kept playing through my mind in an endless loop.

Eventually I decided I just had to try it and see. I thought back to what had filled my fantasies years ago back in my graduate dorm, images of being massaged by strong, firm, older hands, and wrote a description based on those desires. "Smooth boy seeking older man to fondle me – m4m," the headline read, the "m4m" abbreviation specifying it was a man seeking another man. In the post, I was clear that I wanted someone safe who had been recently tested, that I didn't want to be penetrated, that I wanted them to stay clothed, and that I wanted them to play with my bottom and fondle my penis. I took a picture from behind with my knees on the bed, my naked bottom lifted in the air, and my head buried in a pillow. Just to preserve my anonymity, I made the picture black and white and made sure my face wasn't visible.

As I wrote and posted the ad, the fantasy came rushing back to life in my head, as powerful as it had ever been. I masturbated immediately, and once I had cleaned myself up, I went back to the computer to see what responses I'd received. I found the aforementioned flood, and then immediately deleted the ad. So it went, then, over the course of the next few days: posting, masturbating, reading, deleting, until finally the message came in from Zakai.

In his photos, Zakai appeared tall, slim, and well built, grey hair with a moustache and beard that unsettlingly reminded me of somebody in my office building. I didn't find myself drawn to him, but in his message he clearly expressed he was happy to comply with my requests, that he would stay clothed while I undressed, and play with my bottom and cock as I wished. He was a married navy veteran and his wife had a don't ask/don't tell policy about his bisexual encounters, so I trusted his promise of discretion. We messaged back and forth a few times, figuring out a time to meet that evening, and eventually exchanged numbers. More nervous than I'd been in years in calling someone new, I eventually worked up the courage to dial.

"Hello?" I said tentatively.

"Hello, is this Hubert?" he asked (I'd chosen to continue using that misheard name from that first almost-experience long ago).

"Yes, is this Zakai?"

"Yes," I responded, the mundane courtesies of conversational protocol already calming me down.

"So where do you live?" he asked. I was taken aback at the abruptness of his request and felt all my courage drain away.

"Ummm, well, maybe this isn't a good idea," I said quietly, and hung up the phone, my heart racing, kicking myself but also feeling like I'd dodged a bullet.

The phone started ringing a minute later. Of course, I thought to myself, he got my number from my call. I let it a ring a couple of times, considering whether to not answer or even to block the number, but curiosity and desire got the better of me: I picked up the phone.

Before I could say a word, he said, "Don't lose your nerve, Hubert," in a calm and reassuring voice.

I had been prepared to hang up, but this unexpected empathy kept me on the line. "But I'm scared," I responded.

"I know," he said gently, "but if you don't try, how will you ever know?"

That gentleness convinced me, and before I could stop myself I'd given him an address within a block of my building, so I could observe him from nearby on the street and walk away if I sensed any danger.

Less than a half hour later, I was waiting in the shadows on the corner of my block and saw Zakai walk by, looking surprisingly ordinary. He looked just like his photos – younger than I had imagined, a little awkward as he peered around looking for me. I decided he seemed safe, or at least honest in having sent me real pictures, and walked up to introduce myself. We shook hands in an almost instinctual male greeting, which felt weird, and we both laughed at the awkwardness. I took him to my building and we got into the elevator; I hadn't said a word since we met.

"Wow, you're even cuter than in your picture!" he said shyly, lifting his eyes for a moment to smile at me.

I just smiled, but the comment made me uncomfortable. I realized I'd rather he didn't say anything at all, but didn't want to be that direct or that negative so early in the encounter. We walked into my place and I asked him if he'd like some wine.

"Sure," he said, smiling again, and I poured us both a big glass.

He started sipping at his, and after taking a couple of tentative sips, I drained my entire glass.

His eyes widened. "Well okay, then," he said.

"Shall we?" I asked awkwardly, and motioned towards the bedroom; he put his glass down and followed me.

I quickly stripped off my clothes and got onto the bed on my knees, just as in my photo, head pressed into the pillow and bottom high in the area, arching my back and moving my bottom back and forth, already fully erect.

"Well, you just want to get right to it, don't you," he laughed.

Again, I wished he would just stop talking and start touching me. He started slowly stroking my cock from the head to the base, sliding his firm hands along my bottom, stopping just before my anus, and moving forward again.

"Wow, look at how much precum you have," he said, genuinely surprised, "it's literally dripping from you."

It was, and at this point I was genuinely and almost painfully turned on.

"You can touch my bottom too," I said, breathing heavily.

He started stroking my cock again but this time moved his hand all the way up my bottom, firmly pressing my anus but not pushing his way in. Suddenly this was going better than I had expected, and I was eager for more.

"Could you get a little lube for your finger?" I asked with ragged breath.

"Sure," he said, reaching over to the bedside table.

He slowly lubed up my bottom and worked a careful finger in. I moaned and started pushing back and forth against him. As he saw me squirming with pleasure, he pushed his finger further in, curling it to stimulate my prostate, all the while massaging my painfully hard cock with his other hand. I was very turned on, and though this is all I had asked for, I knew I wanted to go even further. I thought about asking him to use a toy, but realized this was one my few chances to feel a cock inside me, and that if I didn't take that chance now it might not ever happen.

"Um, why don't you take your clothes off too?" I asked tentatively. I was breaking my own rules, which was simultaneously scaring and exciting me.

"Okay!" he said with enthusiasm. He quickly pulled off his shirt and stepped out of his pants and underwear. I was surprised to see that his cock and balls were completely shaved, just like mine. I circled my hand around his shaft and stroked gently along its entire length, feeling it harden quickly in my hand. I gingerly kissed the skin around the base of his cock, wanting to put it into my mouth but holding back, knowing I was already going far beyond the boundaries I had set out. I could tell my horniness was rapidly shifting my boundaries, and I was trying my best to keep them in check with what little rational capacity I had left. Besides, what I wanted more than to taste his cock was to feel it inside me.

"Do you want to put on a condom?" I asked quietly, still stroking his semi-rigid cock with my hand.

His eyes widened. "But you were very clear that you didn't want to be penetrated," he said.

"I know, I know, but now I'm really turned on," I gasped.

214

"Well okay, then," he laughed.

I put some lube on my hand and massaged him to a full erection, then slipped the condom on his hard member and put lube on that as well, getting back into position with my head on the pillow. He eased himself slowly inside me.

I had been holding my breath, imagining what it would feel like to finally feel an erect cock inside me. To my surprise, it wasn't at all what I expected: it felt smaller and softer than my dildos had, much less than I had been hoping for. I pushed myself back and forth against him, and he somewhat awkwardly pushed in and out, much more gently and gingerly than I had wanted.

"You can fuck me harder," I said, breathlessly, and he went slightly faster, but still not to my satisfaction.

"Can you get some lube and rub my cock while you're inside me?" I asked.

He tried to reach for the bottle but couldn't get to it from behind me. "I'm not sure I can do that while fucking you," he said, sounding uncertain.

"It's okay," I said, frustrated, "just push inside of me and rub my cock with your hand."

He obliged, and I bucked my hips back and forth, thrusting my cock into his hand as he stroked me, coming forcefully into his fingers and dripping down onto to the bed. I finally relaxed, letting him pull out of me, seeing his erection wane from the corner of my eye. As soon I had come, the reality of the situation came back into sharp focus. I was done, and I wanted him out of my apartment.

"Thank you," I said, curtly. I handed him a tissue to wipe the cum from his hand and started putting my clothes back on, not looking at him. My body language was making it abundantly clear that there would be no reciprocation today. He looked disappointed, but started putting his clothes on as well. I walked him out of my place to the elevator, pressing the button for the lobby. We stood quietly together as it made its slow way to the ground floor.

"That was fun," he said awkwardly.

"Yeah," I said, unconvincingly.

"Well if you want to do it again, you know my number!" he said with a smile.

"Yeah," I said, looking down as I made sure he walked out the door of my building.

I went back to my apartment and paced nervously around my living room, full of anxious questions. What had just happened? Why had I let things get so much farther than I had intended? To my relief, I had still kept things safe – we used a condom, I hadn't even put his cock in mouth, so I calmed myself with the thought that I didn't need to worry about anything. But why had it felt so disappointing? Maybe he just wasn't able to fuck me in the way I wanted? Would somebody else be able to do it better?

More than anything else, two questions kept repeating in my mind. The first was whether it had been inconsiderate to push him out of my apartment as soon as I was satisfied – as a matter of decency I should have at least offered to get him off as well, despite my lack of interest at that point. What bothered me even more, though, was why I had felt absolutely no desire to cuddle with him after sex. Despite all the factors that had varied with my different lovers to date, I always wanted to cuddle and be close with my lovers afterwards, drifting to sleep in each others' arms. With Zakai, I just wanted him to leave.

I didn't call or write to him again the next day or even the next week, but by the time a couple of months had passed I felt like I wanted to give the experience another chance, and felt that Zakai was the safest person I could do it with. I wrote him an email asking if he'd like to repeat our encounter from some weeks ago, expecting he might still be hurt from how I'd ended things the last time. Instead, his response was surprisingly full of masculine bravado.

"Yeah, I think I remember you, you're the boy who I fucked so well you were begging for more! Sure, let's do it again!" he wrote in his reply.

This turned me off completely. No, I thought, that wasn't what happened at all; you weren't satisfying me at all, and I had to ask you to use your other hand to stimulate me, but I wanted to give you another chance. How could we have had such disparate perspectives on the same experience? Or was I being completely unfair, in that I hadn't communicated any of my dissatisfaction to him, and instead just shooed him out of my apartment?

In any case, I knew I didn't want to get together with Zakai again, and never wrote him back. Over the next couple of years, I would occasionally put other posts up on craigslist, but after a few half-hearted email exchanges I would always drop out of the conversation. The fantasy, now experienced, was no longer turning me on in the way it once had, and what I had hoped might be the solution to all of my confusion was not at all what I had expected. In some ways, I was relieved to no longer have this question hanging over me, but in others, I was more confused than ever. If Sylvia with her strap-on didn't really do it for me, nor did Zakai with an actual cock, and nor did Heather, the perfect J. Crew girlfriend, who or what could possibly satisfy me?

Swapping Valentines

"Hi, are you here by yourself?" I asked tentatively, turning to face the athletic dancer with her eyes fixated on the DJ booth. I had been dancing nearby for a few songs now, working up my nerve to talk to her.

"I'm married, if that's what you're asking," she said, turning only briefly to look at me.

"Oh, sorry," I said, a little embarrassed, and was about to go off to dance further away when she turned back towards me.

"But that doesn't mean we're joined at the hip. I mean, we're not monogamous," she said, giving me the tiniest of smiles.

"Oh!" I smiled back.

She introduced herself as Stacey; we chatted a bit about good places to dance in Seattle, and I mentioned an underground Tuesday night event some friends had organized. She was interested, so we exchanged numbers, and I told her I'd let her know next time I went.

I wasn't sure about Stacey's level of interest based on that first interaction, but when I texted her about the event the following week, she enthusiastically agreed to join me, and was already there by the time I arrived.

"This is great, thanks for telling me about it!" with a huge, goofy smile that I would never have imagined on her serious face.

We talked, laughed, and danced together for hours that night, and finally as the last few songs began to play around 2 a.m., I asked her if she might want to hang out sometime.

"You mean tonight?" she asked sincerely, smiling, "I'll have to check..."

"No," I laughed, "not tonight; some other night!"

"Oh, of course," she laughed, "Yes! I would like that," the huge smile again.

It was early November, but I always like to make the first date on neutral ground, so we decided to take a thermos of my homemade mulled wine to Volunteer Park and watch the sunset together. I met her in the park; the weather had turned out to be cold and cloudy and she was in an oversized hoodie, her cheeks adorably red from the cold. We shivered together on the hill and had some of the hot wine, leaning up against each other for warmth, but not quite familiar enough yet to cuddle.

"I know this might seem forward," I said, "but how would you feel about going to my place, just to be warmer? It's freezing out here."

"Oh my god, yes," she laughed, "I was hoping you'd say that."

We walked back to my apartment and sat down on the couch with the rest of the mulled wine. She took off her bulky hoodie to reveal a worn and close-fitting t-shirt that softly followed the contours of her small frame. We were having a great time talking; she was an avid reader like me, and told me about several of the science fiction series she had been devouring recently. When we reached the end of the wine, there was an awkward pause in the conversation, and we leaned in to kiss each other. She was much stronger than I had expected for her size; she pushed herself against my body with a force that was both intense and intoxicating; putting our glasses down, we embraced and kissed passionately.

After a few minutes she asked, "can I take off your shirt?"

I nodded yes and she proceeded to take it off, smiling and stroking appreciatively.

"Oh, this is nice," she said, with that big smile appearing again. Suddenly, she looked at her phone, "Oh no, I have to get to work!" she said and started getting up.

"But wait!" I protested, "can't we take your shirt off too?"

"There's no time!" she laughed, and I had to laugh with her. She ran out the door, kissing me, and promising she'd call me soon.

She called that same evening, apologizing she'd had to run off, and saying how much she enjoyed spending time with me; I told her the same, and we made plans for another get-together the following weekend, this time meeting at my place. I texted her on the way home telling her I was picking up some food for myself at the grocery and asking whether she wanted anything; she replied she hadn't had time for dinner and would appreciate it. I picked up a plate of sushi and some wine and came home with just a few minutes to arrange the nigiri, rolls, wasabi, and soy sauce onto proper platters.

She came in the door and kissed me immediately.

"I got some food for us!" I said between kisses.

"Oh thank you!" she replied, "What did you get?"

"Sushi!" I replied, and gestured at the spread.

"Wow!" she said, "I thought we were just going to eat it out of the box!"

We both laughed, and sat down to eat and drink together, talking and laughing together as easily as we had the previous time, though this time feeling the pull of desire every time our eyes met.

With a couple of pieces left on the plate, she looked over to the side and asked, "is that your bedroom?"

"Yes," I said, blushing.

She jerked her head in that direction and smiled. "Shall we?" she asked coyly.

"Yes," I said eagerly.

She stripped me down to my underwear, hungrily looking my body up and down with her eyes; it felt unexpectedly wonderful to be appreciated in this way. I started taking her clothes off, drawing in my breath as I did – she was of the same slight build as me, but even more toned and muscular than I had expected from our brief makeout session the previous time.

"Wow," I said, and she smiled that big smile again, and we pressed our bodies into each other on the bed.

We kissed and rubbed against each other; her sleek body and mine fit so well together, her scent was intoxicating me, and I couldn't wait to continue further into our exploration of each other. She sat up and began to tug at my underwear, smiling, and I let her slide it down over my legs. I started to do the same with her and she stopped me.

"I have to tell you something," she said. Ah, I thought, perhaps her agreement with her husband is that she can make out with others but not have sex. Her voice quieted down as she said, "I have an injury, and vaginal sex is often really painful for me. I hope that's ok." She looked away, embarrassed.

"Oh, sure, we don't have to have sex," I said quickly, "I'm just enjoying being here with you."

Now she smiled again, "I didn't say we couldn't have sex, silly!" she said, "There are lots of other ways to have sex, you know."

"Oh," I smiled. "Sure, I have a whole box full of sex toys," I said.

"You do!" she laughed with delight, "well let's see them!"

Usually I would never have brought this up so early, but Stacey was different, and after having been vulnerable with me, it was the least I could do. Besides, hiding this had only ended in disaster with Heather, so I figured she might as well find out now. I pulled out my box of butt plugs and dildos; she started looking through it with fascination.

"Oh, you have some good ones here," she laughed, one arm around my waist. I laughed shyly.

"Wait, what's this?" she said, reaching the canvas bag with the leather strap-on harness. "Is this a strap-on?" She said.

"Um, yes," I said, squirming a bit, not yet understanding her reaction.

"Could we try it?" she asked eagerly.

"Sure..." I said, delighted, but not expecting this.

"Now?" she asked, almost pleading.

It was my turn to laugh. "Yes!" I said enthusiastically.

She had worn a strap-on before but hadn't used one with a double buckle system, so I helped her get it adjusted and tightly fastened onto her body, choosing one of my favorite dildos, a green silicone shaft with multiple large ripples.

"Wow, this is a great fit, much better than the one I have," she said.

As we kissed, I lubed up the dildo now mounted firmly to her body, then turned around to bury my face into the pillow with my bottom in the air.

"Oh, YEAH," she said with delight, rubbing lube into my bottom with her firm, strong hands, then sliding the dildo up and down, pressing it gently but firmly against my opening as I quivered with anticipation. She patiently worked in the tip, then the first, then the second, then all the way to the hilt at the third ripple. I felt the fullness I had been craving, and expected that she would now gently (and disappointingly) move it back and forth as my previous strap-on lovers had.

I couldn't have been more wrong. Once inside, she started fucking me *hard*. Her legs were as strong as her arms, and she held on to my hips and stroked deep into me, in and out, just as I had wanted. "Mmm, oh yeah," she kept panting under her breath as she thrusted into me over and over again.

"Mmm, mmm, MMM," I managed to moan. Inadvertently, I was making the sounds I made when I masturbated with the plugs on my own.

She slowed down for a moment to check on me. "Is that too hard?" she asked.

"No," I said breathlessly, it's *perfect*."

"Oh good," she laughed, and continued thrusting into me forcefully. It felt amazing, and I could feel the pre-cum dripping from me; she gathered it in her hand it and used it to lube up my extremely erect cock. After what felt like an hour of intense pleasure, she got some more lube, covered my cock, and stroked it with a tight squeeze while she continue to fuck me; I came harder than I had in months.

Swapping Valentines

"Oh my god," I gasped between breaths, "that was amazing."

She gave me her big goofy smile, and crawled up to kiss me. My body was spent, and I had an urgent need to cuddle with her.

"I know we didn't talk about it," I said shyly, "but could you stay over?"

She looked at the clock. "Well, I'll have to get up at 4:30 to go to work, but if that's OK, I'd love to."

"Yes!" I said.

I quickly cleaned up in the bathroom, then came back to snuggle up into her arms. Our bodies were so perfectly sized for each other, we fell asleep holding each other almost immediately. Her alarm went off as expected at 4:30, and I struggled to get up with her. She pushed me down with a firm hand.

"No, beautiful," she said, "I want you to sleep."

"But I have to get up to lock the door after you!"

"Okay," she smiled, "but you're not allowed to put clothes on, and you have to go right to bed right after."

"I promise," I smiled.

She jumped into her clothes, gave me a passionate kiss, and was gone.

For the next few months we saw each other at least twice a week. The sex was always amazing; many nights I would bring her to orgasm with my hand before or after she fucked me. I loved seeing her tight body contract, her powerful abs bulging as her body shuddered into the heights of pleasure and then relax. It was more than just sex, though – we would cuddle up to watch movies together, go to poetry readings, venture out to late night diners, spend hours perusing used bookstores. Her work schedule was unpredictable and we took whatever time we could, always trying to spend the night together when possible.

When Valentine's day came around and she was complaining about how forced and ridiculous the whole thing was, an idea popped into my head.

"What if we did a reverse valentine's, flipping the traditional gender roles on their heads?" I asked.

She looked at me with a quizzical expression, tilting her head to the side. "What do you mean?" she asked.

"Well," I said, "I'll wear a dress, and you'll wear a suit, and when you come home from work I'll have dinner ready, and then you'll take me in the bedroom and fuck me silly."

She laughed, "Ha! Yes! That sounds amazing! I can wear the suit you tailored for me!" "Exactly," I said with a smile.

Swapping Valentines

I hadn't dressed in drag since the incident in Belltown, but Stacey was special, and I wanted to make it perfect. I found a slim red dress at a used clothing store, spent the time to tailor it perfectly to my body, and the night of the fourteenth I paired it with a short blond wig and red lipstick. Stacey came through the door in her suit and hat, and her eyes widened at my outfit.

"Wow, that wig really works on you. And that dress!" she said, then grabbed me in her strong arms to kiss me.

We barely made it through dinner and rushed into the bedroom; she slid off my dress and pulled off her outfit to reveal she was already wearing her own strap-on and dildo.

"Tonight let's try something different," I said, and instead of burying my head in the pillow, I lay back on the bed, bringing my knees to my chest.

"Oh, I like this," she smiled, and climbed on top of the bed and reached of the lube. I was extremely turned on – the setup, the position, everything together had me an unexpected state.

"Could you, um..." I started.

"What," she asked, her eyes full of desire.

"Could you, um.... lick my bottom?" I felt embarrassed even asking, but I was too turned on to stop myself.

Her eyes lit up with desire. "Are you sure?" she asked. "I do want to respect your boundaries." She had asked me herself early in our relationship – at that time, I had quietly demurred, too shy to admit how much I wanted her to. This night felt very different.

"Yes," I said, "I'm very sure."

"OK then!" she smiled, pushing my legs up, and beginning by licking up and down from my perineum to the tip of my anus.

I had expected her to just lightly lick my hole with her tongue, but as was often the case with Stacey, my expectations were all wrong. She began that way, artfully flicking her tongue around the edges, which felt heavenly, but then suddenly pushed her tongue deep inside me. I had never felt anything like this before, and with my lubed penis in her hand, it was all I could do to not cum immediately. She kept at it for several blissful minutes, feeling my entire body squirm with pleasure, then before I could say a word leapt her body up to mine to kiss me, pushing her tongue deep into my mouth, letting me taste myself as she continue to stroke my cock. At the same time, she carefully guided her lubed cock into my bottom with her hand. I came immediately and hard as we joyfully collapsed onto each other.

Swapping Valentines

A few weeks later I got a call from Stacey when I was on the way to the gym. It was unusual for her to call and not text, so I picked up immediately.

"What's up, Stacey?" I said.

"Su, I feel like I should tell you that I'm getting a divorce." She paused. "It's not because of you or anything, I don't want you to worry about that, I just want you to know." She paused again; this was unusual for her. "And I also wanted to tell you that I love you; I have for a while and I just haven't been able to say it. You don't have to say it back or anything, I just wanted to tell you."

"Oh," I said, thrown off guard. "I love you too, Stacey!" In my awkward inability to handle silence, I added, "I've been thinking of you as my girlfriend already!"

She paused again. "I don't think that's true, Su; just last week you said you want a girlfriend who's monogamous, and you were still looking for that."

"Oh, um, er, yeah," I said sheepishly.

"Well anyway," she said, sounding a little tired now, "I just wanted to let you know; I don't want that to make it weird or anything."

"Okay, sure," I said.

"I'll talk to you soon," she said, and hung up.

I kept walking, wondering what this meant. I was used to Stacey being in a primary relationship with her husband; I hadn't even thought about the possibility of a long-term relationship with her. Did I want that? Our chemistry was so amazing, both in and out of the bedroom, why shouldn't I? But what about the sex thing? Would I be ok with never being able to have vaginal sex with her? And she wasn't at all like the J. Crew fantasies of my youth. But look where things went with Heather, that didn't work at all. But even if I did want to be with her, would she be willing to be monogamous? Did it matter? I couldn't stop thinking about all of this, and it occupied me for the days and weeks ahead.

As much as we hadn't wanted it to happen, things did become weird. We saw each other less and less frequently, and while sex was always a part of our earlier meetings, it became less and less common on our dates. Eventually she called out how it seemed like we were drifting apart, and perhaps it would be better for us to just be friends than lead ourselves into a messy breakup. I agreed, and we continued to hang out as friends a few more times, and then rapidly lost touch with each other. We would occasionally comment on each others' photos on social media, but even that became rare as time went on.

More than a decade after those nights I still think about Stacey, her wide, goofy smile, and our many happy moments together in and out of the bedroom. Once when going through our old photos I found a video I had recorded of her fucking me, long before things started falling apart. I had set up the camera in the bedsheets, and it managed to capture her lubing up her dildo and my eager bottom as I moved back and forth against her hand before it fell over onto the bed from the motion. As she grabbed my hips and began to enter me, she picked up the camera to point it down at the dildo as she entered me, then as she slid in and out, in and out as my hips moved against hers. She then set it back down on the bedspread and started fucking me energetically. The camera promptly fell over again and all you could see in the video was the dark red of my sheets, but the audio captured every moment – our inadvertent sounds of pleasure as she thrust into me again and again, her exertion and excitement as she bucked her hips against mine. When she stopped thrusting to get more lube to cover my cock, she noticed the camera had fallen, and propped it up again, so it had a clear view of her last few thrusts as she stroked me to a shuddering orgasm all over her eager hand.

The entire video is incredibly hot, despite its grainy footage and comical camerawork, but what makes my heart skip a beat every time is what happened next. As I came, we both took a few ragged breaths of exertion and pleasure, and then I started laughing, and she started laughing, and suddenly we were both laughing with all our bodies, a sound of unbridled, unmistakable, harmonious joy until the moment the video cuts out.

It has taken me the perspective of all the years before and after then to recognize how pure and special that was. At the time, though, it was just one joyful moment out of so many with Stacey, and I had no doubt there would be countless more to come. Caught up in my long-held notions of what the perfect relationship should look like, with far too little perspective on the rareness of that feeling, I let that flame go out as suddenly and unexpectedly as it had appeared.

A Party for Unicorns

Walking into the apartment, I realized this was not the party I had expected. I knew from the invite that my friend Caleb was celebrating his 25th birthday and it was going to be a unicorn-themed party. Furthermore, Caleb always brought fun and levity to any situation he entered, from the "lingerie party" where we met, to a friend's dog's funeral (unexpectedly), so I was expecting no matter what it would be a good time.

I had assumed, though, that our usual crowd was going to attend – instead, I was surprised to see it was only his male friends and lovers, in what was quickly becoming a no-holds-barred make-out party. While there were plenty of beautiful boys there, and it could have been the perfect opportunity to try another experience with a man, nobody was catching my fancy. I poured myself a sizable drink and sank down into a big couch, facing the door, wondering if I should just call it a night and head home.

A Boy Named Su

I was still staring at the door when it suddenly opened to reveal a lanky, short-haired woman, popped collar denim jacket above a faded, body-hugging t-shirt, Carhartt pants, and work boots. Her bright blue eyes narrowed below her shiny, swept-up hair as she looked around the party, grimacing. I was immediately attracted to her but her style and presence at the party made me fairly certain she was not interested in men; still, I couldn't stop staring.

She saw me looking, stared back, and started walking purposefully towards me, still grimacing. I thought she was going to call me out for staring and prepared myself to apologize, but instead she dropped down on to couch right next to me, staring forward, not saying a word. For a few agonizing minutes we sat there in silence as I waited to see what would happen. Eventually I turned, thinking I would start by introducing myself, but seeing my motion she turned at the same time and moved her body towards mine; our eyes locked and the mutual desire was strangely and surprisingly clear.

We locked our mouths into a kiss, our arms quickly following to pull each other in. Her kisses were as hungry as mine, but more ferocious; she used her teeth and her tongue to press further and deeper into my mouth than I was comfortable with, but I was too drawn to her to stop. I felt moments of pain, but the pleasure of our connection outweighed it by a large margin, and to my surprise it was adding to my desire.

A Party for Unicorns

There were still dozens of other people at the party, but either nobody paid any attention to us or at least we didn't notice that they did; the world was just our mouths, our arms, and our bodies.

After a few minutes I started to draw back to take a breath and talk to her, but she held me in with her arm, our foreheads touching, both breathing heavily.

"Do you live alone?" she asked between breaths, still not releasing her hold.

"Yeah, I'm just a few blocks away," I said.

"OK. Good. Here's the deal. I want you to take me home and fuck me like you fuck the boys," she said.

"Well, I don't really fuck boys..." I started to say.

"Whatever," she said curtly, cutting me off. "I know what you are. Let's go, before I change my mind."

I didn't know quite how to respond, but knew I was incredibly attracted to her and would follow her wherever she wanted to go, do whatever she wanted to do. She got up from the couch and grabbed my hand, not so much in a romantic gesture, but to pull me along with her. We walked out of the party; as we left I saw Caleb blissfully making out with three lovely boys. I saw no point in disturbing him to say goodbye, especially given the speed with which we were heading out the door. As we got out onto the street I made an attempt at introduction; I told her my name was Su.

"You can call me Dar," she said with a quick smirk.

We walked the five blocks to my place in near silence, and as soon as we got in the door she asked, "Where's your bedroom?" – more of a command than a question. She pulled me in the room and rapidly stripped off all of her clothes. Though I had been drawn to her at the party, I was breathless at the sight of her naked body – she was exactly my type, slender and athletic, long limbs and high shoulders, with a beautiful face that had lost the hard edge of the party and was now beckoning to me. As I was taking my clothes off, she got onto the bed, putting her forearms and head down into the pillow and her tiny bottom into the air. It was a pose I had taken all too many times myself, and I couldn't stop but stare, both marveling at her loveliness and the juxtaposition of roles.

"Now fuck me like you fuck the boys, c'mon," she said, her voice still commanding, but now underlined with desire.

I put on a condom and got up on the bed behind her, stroking her lovely hips and legs, pulling her towards me by her hipbones. As my cock pressed up against her vulva, I could feel that it was already wet, and I started to slowly rub against it.

A Party for Unicorns

"NUH-UH, NO WAY, not in there," she called out, "I want you to fuck me like you fuck the *boys*," she said, almost hissing out the last word.

"I mean, like I said, that's not really what I do, I mostly date women..." I tried to explain again.

"Shut up, and just do it," she cried, and then, in a quieter voice, almost pleading, "don't make me lose my nerve."

I put some lube on my hands and started to gently finger her beautiful bottom, sliding up and down in the groove between her cheeks, feeling her pushing her small body into my hand. I inserted a tip of my finger inside her and held it there; she made an inadvertent "mmm" that sounded remarkably like mine. I started to work more of the finger in, sliding it in and out the way I liked doing to myself; her lithe body started to squirm and she lifted one of her hands to her vulva and started rubbing herself.

"Do it!" she hissed, her voice heavy with desire.

I started to push the head of my cock gingerly into her bottom, knowing from years of experience that a sudden stretch could be painful; I didn't want to ruin the moment.

"Is this ok?" I asked tentatively.

"Yes," she gasped, squirming, "more, MORE."

I pressed in further until the head slipped in; she made a slight gasp and for a moment I worried I had pushed too hard, but she was squirming and bucking her hips up against me. I started to make gentle, slow strokes, pulling myself into her hips, a little bit more each time until I was completely inside her.

"Is this all right?" I asked tentatively.

"YES," she responded, "fuck me, FUCK ME!"

I continued with the slow strokes, now going from tip to hilt, and watching her carefully, worried that I might hurt her by going too fast.

"HARDER!" she yelled out, and I complied, but still carefully. The last person I had fucked in this way was Sylvia, and when I went all out she stopped me just before I came as it was hurting her; I didn't want to repeat that experience, especially with someone I had just met.

Eventually she started convulsing in my hands, "Right there, hold it RIGHT THERE!" she yelled, as she buried her face in the pillow and made muffled sounds I wished I could have heard in their entirety. Her entire body arched in, then out, then in again as she shuddered to an orgasm and collapsed. She breathed heavily for a moment with her face in the pillow and then turned to face me with her signature smirk.

"Okay, your turn," she said, "get on the bed, NOW."

I got into the position she had been in a minute ago; she lubed up my bottom and started moving her finger inside me. She had no qualms about gentleness; she pushed in hard with one finger and quickly two, then pushed and stroked me inside my rectum, towards my prostate. It was intense but I was loving it; I bucked my body against her hand for some time, then moved one my hands to my cock to start stroking, already feeling the precum collecting in my hand. When she saw me doing that, she batted my hand away.

"Not yet," she said curtly.

I dutifully put my hand back down, feeling the intensity of her stimulation for what felt like ages of blissful agony, wanting so much to touch myself. "Ok, now," she said, and I gladly lubed up my cock and started stroking it; she started pushing down harder towards my prostate, and within moments I had come all over the sheets.

"Wow," she remarked, sounding genuinely surprised. "You're much more of a bottom than a top, aren't you?" With that, she walked off to the bathroom to clean up.

I breathed heavily, face still in the pillow, thinking about what she said. Was I? I certainly loved being fucked, but I loved fucking as well. Did she say that because I was too gentle? But I just hadn't wanted to hurt her, I argued to myself. Then I thought back to the times when past lovers or even Zakai had seemed too careful and how frustrated I had felt; suddenly I felt a wave of empathy for all of them. Still, I should have been more like Stacey, fucking athletically and enthusiastically, I thought to myself. But I barely know this person, and how awful would it have been if I had hurt her?

All these thoughts were playing through my mind as Dar came back from the bathroom. I opened the shades; the early summer sun was already streaming in – we must have been playing with each other for hours. I stood up and started to put my clothes back on.

"Don't," she said with a smile, "I like you better this way."

She gave me a hard kiss, again biting the outside of my mouth and shoving her tongue deep inside my mouth, grabbing and stroking my cock with her hand.

"Wow, this is the first time I've been with a boy since I was a teenager," she said, almost to herself. "It's kinda fun!" she continued, with a mischievous grin. "Here," she commanded, handing me her phone, "put your number in there so I can call you when I feel like doing this again."

I happily complied, excited that there might be a next time when I could fuck her the way she really wanted, the way I wanted, when she could try out my strap-ons, and who knows what else. I awkwardly pulled out my phone as well, out of habit, as I was the one usually taking down a number. I put my name and number into her phone, then handed her phone back and put mine back on the shelf.

Her face fell. "You put your phone away?" she asked. "Don't you want my number too?"

"Sure, well, I just thought... you said you'd call me..." I stammered.

"Whatever," she said, eyes downcast and looking away, "I have to go anyway."

Suddenly the tough-as-nails Dar looked rejected and upset; I wanted to talk to her, explain to her, cuddle with her, and most of all see her again, but before I opened my mouth again she lifted her face back up, and the hard shell she had worn when I first saw her was back.

"I have to go," she said grimly, and walked rapidly for the door.

I jumped up to follow her and said, "Hold on, I'll walk out with you."

"I can see my own way out," she say brusquely, then looked down at my still naked body and said, "besides, you're not even wearing any pants," giving me a tiny shadow of her confident smirk. And with that, she was gone.

I went back to sit on my bed. What had just happened? I was overwhelmed by so many conflicting feelings, most of all regret at how I had handled those last few minutes. I had broken through her shell, she had reached out to me, and unwittingly I had rejected her. But she didn't even give me a chance to explain, I argued back to myself. Still, she must have been in a very vulnerable place, having not been with boys at all for all those decades. And what about this question of being a bottom vs. a top? Was I really more of a bottom? But I loved being the one on top as well – didn't I?

I wanted desperately to contact her, to see her again, even just to talk about all of this, but had no idea how to reach her. Since her name was fairly unusual, I looked online for hours, hoping to find a mention of her somewhere. Eventually I found a twitter account with her first name; her profile picture didn't have her face. When I saw her latest tweet, from what must have been just minutes after leaving my place, I was sure it was her. "What the hell just happened?" it read. Indeed.

Given how things had ended between us, now reinforced by that tweet, I sensed she didn't want to see me again, and never reached out to her. To this day, I think back often to that experience: she had seen me, through all the layers of my male costume, perhaps to a greater degree than she even realized. I had seen her, despite her own costume, from the moment she walked in the door. We had held each other, intensely connected with each other, exchanging barely a word.

How rare and how wonderful that we could find each other in such an unexpected place. How kind of fate to let us see each other's desire at the same moment and make that unlikely leap into each other's arms. And yet, how careless we were to just let it fade away into a summer morning.

A Boy Named Su

The Pit and the Pendejo

Nobody said it was easy
Oh it's such a shame for us to part
Nobody said it was easy
No one ever said it would be so hard –
I'm going back to the start...

Just a few short weeks before, Gabrielle had excitedly shared Coldplay's "The Scientist" with me; now the mournful lines resonated through the silence inside the car, as though every word were underlined. Gabrielle switched it off with a rapid flick of her wrist, mumbling "why are we listening to this sad music right now."

She glanced over at me with a worried look. We were on the way to pick up her four-year-old daughter, Newt, and I had been crying for at least three hours. I had been crying when we got in the car, I had been crying when we checked out of the beautiful in-city resort she had booked for us for the weekend, I had been crying when we packed up our things, I had been crying as I took a shower, I had been crying while we were still naked together in bed.

It took me years to fully understand what had happened just before. I remember getting incredibly upset about something she had said about our lovemaking, something that wasn't a big deal, but unlocked this geyser of tears that wouldn't stop for hours. Five months later she sent me her photos from that night, but I wouldn't open them until long after we had parted ways; the memory of that night was still too painful. When I eventually opened the folder, more than eight years later, I found not only photos but a few videos, including an accidental clip of the moments just before the tears. We were in bed: naked, talking, cuddling, kissing. The first few times I tried to watch it I stopped it a few seconds in, immediately critical of my own behavior. My voice was high, even higher than my usual register – silly, soft, and sweet, almost baby talk, gentle, happy words interspersed with kisses and snuggles – and I was disgusted to see myself acting that way.

I was disgusted to see myself acting that way.

It took me a few times to notice that, and when I finally did, I asked myself why. "It's just not masculine," I thought, "why couldn't I have been..." Oh. Of course.

The Pit and the Pendejo

As I had started to do more and more often, I asked myself how I would have judged that behavior if it had been a woman saying and doing the same things instead of me. As I mulled it over, I realized I would have found it sweet and adorable, just the sort of lover *I* would want to have. I also realized why I had felt that visceral reaction to seeing myself this way, and how fragile I was about it being noticed.

It was only then that I could re-hear the words from her that I had blocked out of my mind for so many years – "sometimes when we make love, I'm not really turned on." She followed this with practical suggestions of how I might be able to improve things, some of it focused on that tone of voice. In retrospect, I don't think she was intentionally making any kind of comment about my masculinity, but this had touched a deep-seated fear in me from when we first met, and it was hard for me not to see it this way.

To understand why, I needed to go back even further, to the rainy mountaintop where we met two years beforehand, where some friends were throwing an underground rave. The relentless rain had been unexpected and most of us huddled under whatever shelter we could find. I was standing under a pop-up tent and she was just outside it, sheltering herself with a thin umbrella. I was certain that she was the loveliest woman I had ever seen, tall and narrow in a thin hoodie, with brilliant blue eyes that shone even in the dreary grey of the mountain rain.

"Come in, come in out of the rain," I called out to her. She gave me a tiny but friendly smile and came inside the covered area to stand beside me.

We had a brief but intense conversation, and being nervous, I talked far too much; in trying to connect with her I told her about the recent experience I'd had with spanking. I talked about how it had opened my mind to how things I hadn't considered pleasurable could in fact be, that it was a matter of perspective and trying new things. I had meant it as an example of exploring desire and intimacy, but she seemed taken aback. She excused herself with a smile, saying, "uh, good luck with all of that..."

I was certain I had said too much and had ruined my chances, but I kept searching for her that night and was distraught at being unable to find her again (unbeknownst to me, she had left the party shortly afterwards for unrelated reasons). For the next year, I would run into her unexpectedly at events around town, and eventually we became friends on social media. Then came the incredibly sweaty night at Neumo's, the hottest Seattle had seen in a decade, when while slamming our drenched bodies together to the intoxicating beats of the Glitch Mob we simultaneously said to each other, "we should spend more time together!"

The Pit and the Pendejo

Though we both had planned to take it slow, we ended up spending the night together on our very first date. Our chemistry was intense even on that first night; in the years afterwards I was always amazed by how consistently the sight of her face, the touch of her skin, or even a fleeting kiss could turn me on. However, I was in an unexpected moment of plenty: I had more dates (and potential dates) than I could handle, and still reeling from my experience with Heather, I was deeply skeptical of long-term relationships. Gabrielle told me she was comfortable with my seeing whoever I wanted to as long as we could still see each other. Still, I felt the sense of a relationship closing in on me, and as she would many times in the future, she intuited my thoughts on this. "Don't worry about what's going to happen in the future," she wrote to me in a text message, "let's just spend time with each other as long as it makes us happy, and let go if it no longer does."

It was exactly what my nervous heart needed to hear, and without telling her I quickly ended all my other dating relationships. In less than a month we were spending four to five nights together every week, and it became difficult to imagine weekends without her. While I always valued my alone time, for the first time in my life, I slept far better with someone in my arms than I did on my own, and looked forward to weekends when we would be sharing space for all the hours of the day and night. The sex was incredible (for me), but it was the cuddles and casual intimacy that warmed my heart in the way I had always longed for.

Newt, her shy little four-year old, also became a fast friend; I first broke the ice with my Elmo puppet, and for a few weeks she would only talk to me through him. Before long, though, I started keeping Elmo in my backpack, telling her he got lost on the bus. Eventually she decided I was okay to talk to as well, at least when Elmo wasn't around. She loved my silliness and I loved hers; I rapidly began to think of the three of us as a happy little family. I loved them both so much and desperately wanted this to become the fairytale ending I had always dreamed of. I pulled my cis het male costume around me more tightly than I ever had before, determined to make it work.

From the earliest days, though, there were warning signs. Gabrielle generally wouldn't comment on my feminine mannerisms in our one-on-one interactions, but often when we were out with others she would say things about my behavior or style. A brief mention that her cousins "didn't know what to think" when they saw my pointy boots, that "it was weird how I always had to hug *all* of my friends," or when her father mocked my "girliness" she laughed instead of defending me. Looking back at some photos in groups I notice her seeming almost embarrassed of me in a few shots when I was dressed particularly flamboyantly.

The Pit and the Pendejo

There was the other side of this coin, too – when she expressed an interest in attending college, the rest of her family, who had never gone, tried to talk her out of it. I took the side of her ambition, gently encouraging her when she lost her nerve, passionately arguing why it would be a good choice when she was feeling more confident. I helped her get her applications together and then with her homework and financial aid once she started. She was always extremely appreciative and would become extra soft when I would help her in this way.

Still, I always felt she longed to see a more masculine side of me. I remember her listening in one evening while I was on a work call, and saying, "Wow, you must be a totally different, hardcore person at work, I've never seen that side of you," with a look of admiration in her eyes. On the one hand I found this flattering, but on the other, I grimaced, feeling (perhaps unfairly) a criticism of my lack of "hardcoreness" in our daily life. But this was not how I wanted to be with her – I wanted to be tender, soft, and sweet, and for the most part she seemed to love my affection, returning it in her own sweet way day after day and night after night.

Though we had both expected the worst, those hours of crying on that car ride did not end our relationship. That was only six months in, and we stayed together for another year and half, becoming stronger and stronger together with each passing month and year.

In our fateful last summer together, though, without warning and almost overnight, she suddenly became distant. We would still sleep together but she wouldn't want to cuddle, and at dinner or breakfast she would barely talk. Our warmth and intimacy had been the bedrock of our relationship, and without I felt like the ground was crumbling beneath us. I would ask her what was wrong and she would always say "nothing's wrong," only growing irritated at my questions. I cried to myself when she was away, as I felt us growing further and further apart, not knowing what to do.

In the last month of our relationship, we took a vacation with Newt to Ocean Shores in Oregon, a lovely seaside tourist town with wide beaches and friendly local restaurants. We had been having a hard time communicating with each other, and on one of the last nights, in a tiny pizza parlor, she was completely engrossed in her phone. I used the time to talk and joke with Newt, who despite her youth was extremely sensitive to the tensions between Gabrielle and myself, and had grown steadily quieter over the course of the trip.

Suddenly Gabi looked up from her phone to ask, "so why do you shave your armpits anyway?" in a tone that was not at all friendly.

I turned white. "It's, uh, something I've done since, uh, I was a swimmer in grad school – uh, lots of swimmers do it," I managed to stammer out.

The Pit and the Pendejo

She turned away and started sobbing, and I didn't know what to do. Newt looked extremely upset, and I tried to comfort both her and her mother, but Gabi was inconsolable. I reached out a hand to hold her shoulder and she batted it away, something she had never done. "Don't TOUCH ME!" she yelled.

"I'm so sorry," I said, shocked, "I was just trying to help."

"Just forget it," she said, wiping away her tears and turning back to her phone.

In some sense I had dreaded this moment for a long time. I had, in fact, shaved my armpits since graduate school, not so much because they improved my swimming times, but because they felt more sexy to me when smooth. I always felt lucky that I had very little hair on my body apart from my head – though most of the men in my family are exceptionally hairy, I am quite the opposite. Beyond a few scraggly remnants on my legs my only other hair is in my armpits and my pubic region. When not dating, I often shave all of this away, as I love the feeling of smoothness; for Gabrielle, I had left a small fermata above my cock, but more than once I felt her running her hand around the area, as if wondering what was missing.

Pendejo, I've learned since then, literally translates to "pubic hair," and in retrospect I can see how much like Poe's hapless character in the "Pit and the Pendulum" I was. Strapped to that table, I held my breath, in wait for those two signs of my masculinity gone wrong, the pit and pendejo, swinging ever closer, until that conversation.

Things were never the same again after that trip. Shortly afterwards, she began talking about a friend of hers who she was worried about but had lost touch with, and nearly all our conversations started revolving around him. Eventually she regained contact with him and started canceling our weekend plans so that she could spend time with him.

"Are you sleeping with him?" I asked, not so much as an accusation, more just wanting to know where we were in our relationship.

"No way! He's missing half of his teeth, I'm not going to sleep with him. I just want to make sure he's OK." It felt like she was protesting too much, but I wanted to give her the benefit of the doubt. This went on for a few weeks, until eventually one night she came over to calmly tell me that "maybe right now we're just better apart."

I was devastated but I didn't want to show it; I tried to move on with my life and get back to the carefree single world I had inhabited so happily in the past. Instead I fell into a downward spiral; at a birthday party in the mountains with friends, I drank too much, passed out in the bathroom, and broke a couple of teeth in the process. I am thankful it wasn't something worse; the pain of that experience and the year of dental reconstruction that followed snapped me out of that space and back to life. Still, the level of cynicism about relationships I gained during that time would be hard for me to shake for many years afterwards.

More than a decade has passed now and we are friends again; it's good to see her and Newt, and sometimes we'll talk a bit about old times, though I feel we have very different perspectives on the ending. A year or two ago, at a summer festival, I ran into someone who recognized me – I didn't recognize him, but when he asked me about Gabrielle I noticed the toothless gaps in his smile.

"How do you know Gabrielle?" I asked.

"Oh, you know, we used to date," he said candidly. "That's why her boyfriend doesn't like me, it's because I had sex with her, you know." He laughed at the last bit.

I smiled and nodded; it only confirmed what I had long suspected. Seeing him, I understood further – he was masculine in all the ways that I was not – dirty, carefree, rough, tall; I understood now, and this many years afterwards, it was (mostly) no longer hurtful.

I had lunch with Gabrielle a few months afterwards and told her I had met the toothless friend she had been searching for so desperately in those last weeks of our relationship.

"Oh, how's he doing?" she said.

"Oh, he's great!" and then tentatively, "He told me you used to date."

Her face went blank, eyes darting back and forth across mine, a motion that was all too familiar to me. "Oh, no... then you're talking about a different guy... uh, yeah, that's Jeff, he's also missing some teeth."

"Oh, ok," I said. She had never been a good liar, and there was nothing to be gained from forcing the truth out of her. I smiled and we continued our lunch, parting as always as good friends.

To tell it this way, though, leaves out a critical part of the story. There was a moment of extreme vulnerability early on in our relationship when she told me about a traumatic experience in her childhood, so shocking and unjust I wanted to lash out at the people that could have done this to her, despite her having forgiven them. She had never talked about this with me before, and rather than telling me she had given me a slim journal with a series of writings about the two of us, with this painful story embedded in the midst of it.

It was a moment of openness that I could have used to share my own vulnerability, to tell of her of the experiences that shaped me, the identity I was struggling to find between the masculine and the feminine, the source behind the shaved pits, the pendejo, the soft voice, the cutesy mannerisms. But I did not. I comforted her, I raged on her behalf, I spoke out against the injustice of what happened – but I never had the courage to be vulnerable with her in the way she was with me.

In the music video for "the Scientist," you're walked backwards in time from a city street to the scene of a disaster, and every moment you're cringing as you know the terrible moment is approaching. At first the character is isolated in a world that moves on without him, then he's running backwards through the woods, then there's a horrific car accident, but only at the very end do you see it all comes from an innocent moment, when his lover takes off her seatbelt to put her jacket back on, a split second before a logging truck causes them to swerve off the narrow road and into the disaster that follows.

> *Tell me your secrets*
> *And ask me your questions*
> *Oh let's go back to the start...*

Today, then, I wonder – how different might it have been if I had been brave about my truth and acted differently in that moment? What if the pendulum had not finally cut us apart in that pizzeria, or a year earlier in that morning of tears, but all the way at the start when we were first revealing the nakedness of our inner selves to each other? Had I set the disaster in motion myself when I wouldn't open up my whole truth to her, whatever her reaction might have been?

Pajamas

"Su!" Casey said, suddenly appearing in front of me, smiling brightly and batting her long eyelashes. "I was hoping I'd see you, I've been thinking about you!"

We were at a massive dance party in a tiny South Seattle venue; I could barely hear her over the wall-to-wall people and the music blaring from two competing sound stages. Even with all the doors open and the freezing temperatures outside, this crowded spot near the doorway was the only part of the venue cool enough to breathe in.

"Oh yeah?" I asked, appreciating the attention, but not sure whether to take her seriously.

"Do you wanna hang out sometime?" she continued.

I was flattered, a little bemused, and not entirely convinced. I'd had a bit of a crush on Casey for years, but she was strictly polyamorous, always dating several people at once, and I hardly thought she'd be interested in someone like me.

Furthermore, her other boyfriends, some of them friends of mine, were quite traditionally male, and I didn't see myself as her type.

"Can I have your number?" she asked hopefully.

"Of course!" I responded, and we exchanged numbers before she left with one of her partners. Despite my doubts, the unexpected interaction left me with a smile on my face.

It had been a good night – I had met a lovely woman while dancing, and later in the evening a lesbian friend with whom I had been talking about my dating misadventures made an unexpected observation: "You know," she said, "you're beautiful like a man and a woman at the same time. Like Prince!"

I was taken off-guard, as she had never said anything like this before. "Maybe I could help you explore the woman side of that," she said with a flirty look. My ears perked up and I turned to see if she was serious, but she quickly followed with, "but I shouldn't, my girlfriend would get mad," with a coy smile.

I smiled back, appreciating the compliment and being seen. It wasn't the first time that I'd heard this; even some very straight male friends with little knowledge of the LGBTQIA+ spectrum had remarked how there were aspects of both the masculine and the feminine in my appearance and behavior. Given the disastrous results of holding on to my male costume too tightly in my previous relationships, I had begun to express myself a little more openly. It was reassuring to hear that at least my friends were beginning to see the real me.

I didn't see Casey again until that summer, this time at a clothing-optional camping festival a few hours north of the city. I had been having a frustrating day – after too many drinks in the hot sun, I'd passed out from the heat, causing my friends a great deal of concern and myself a great deal of embarrassment. I had come back to our camp and was lounging around, just drinking water and more than ready for the day (and the festival) to end.

From the corner of my vision, I saw Casey walking up to me, her shark onesie stripped down to her waist from the heat, her lovely naked body glistening in the late afternoon sun. Earlier she and some other shark-costumed friends had been chasing me and my campmates about in a silly "shark attack." Her friends had left now, her costume was down, and she came up to me slowly and shyly.

"Su," she said, "I really want to spend some time with you. I know before I said I wanted to but then I never called, but I really do," she looked down, a little embarrassed.

Unlike the moment at the party, this time I could tell she was being sincere. "I'd like that too, Casey," I said.

She looked up with a big smile, "Really?" she said. "That's GREAT!" I laughed at her exuberance. "So, do you want to go on a date with me?" she asked, twisting her body and batting her eyelashes playfully.

"Yes; yes I would," I said dramatically, with a theatrical bow.

"HOORAY!!" she cried, making me smile again. She looked down for a bit, and then right at me, asking, "Um, Su, can I have a kiss, before I go?"

I nodded vigorously. She came close, held my hand, and kissed me, a soft and sweet kiss with an intensity that surprised me; her eyes were still closed when we parted. "Thank you," she said quietly, then ran off to find her friends again.

When we came back to Seattle I was excited to make plans with her, texting her a few times over the course of the next weeks with possible dates. While she would always respond sweetly a day or two later, we were never able to find a time. I began to think that she didn't have time for me after all, and chalked up that lovely summer day to just something she was feeling in the literal heat of the moment.

Then, in early November, out of the blue, she called me, asking if I wanted to go see a pop art exhibit with her that very night. I didn't have plans and agreed, thinking we'd finally have a chance to spend some time together. When I arrived, I saw several other male friends had also been invited, and from

Pajamas

their behavior it was clear I wasn't the only one with a little crush on Casey. I decided she just liked having the attention of multiple men, and while I wasn't that interested in more outings like that, I figured that as long as I was there I might as well have fun. We went through the exhibits, took silly photos, played games, and parted ways with friendly hugs. It was a fun evening, but also the last I expected to spend with Casey.

In the next few weeks, though, I began to hear from her at unexpected moments. The first time it happened, I was on a trip to visit my sister out of state, and got a call from her late at night. She was flirty, curious, and talkative, and we had a delightful hours-long conversation, ranging from stuffed animals to our favorite poets. A week after coming back into town, she called to ask what I was doing, and when I said I was hosting a small poetry recitation of my friends' favorite poets, she asked if she could come and was a delightful companion for the evening. Still, I felt that she just wanted to be friends and occasionally get some flirty attention. This was fine with me, but I had resolved to not take her interest too seriously.

About a month later, I had just gone to bed when I got a call from her. "Hello?" I said, surprised to be hearing from her and especially this late.

"Su, could I sleep over at your house tonight?" she asked in a voice that was almost pleading.

I was completely taken by surprise, and wondering if I felt ready to have sex with someone I'd had so little intimacy with thus far. Something in her voice, though, told me this was not about lust, but rather her reaching out for my company.

"Uh, sure, Casey," I said.

"Just so you know, there's not going to be any sex or anything," she said gruffly.

"That's completely fine," I said, relieved, but not surprised.

Then in a softer tone, she continued, "I'm just feeling lonely and abandoned, and I thought of you and thought it would be nice to spend the night with you."

"Sure," I said, touched that she would reach out to me for comfort.

She paused for a second. "Su, is this a bad idea?"

"No," I said immediately, "I'd really like it if you came over."

"Okay," she said, sounding relieved. "I'll be there in half an hour. Will you wait up for me?"

"Of course," I said.

I quickly cleaned up my place as best I could, and before making much progress she arrived in my lobby. I let her upstairs, and as soon as she entered she said, "Oh Su," put her arms around me, and gave me a very long hug. I held her, feeling the weight of her emotions in that moment.

"OK," she said, finally releasing me, "let's get ready for bed."

She brushed her teeth and carried a stuffed animal she'd brought with her to bed, taking her thin t-shirt off but keeping her underwear on. I did the same, nestling up against her, holding her small body in my arms. She gathered my arms around her and said, "Good night, Su," and in minutes was asleep. I was still too charged from the unexpected events to go to sleep, and wondered for a moment how tonight had come to pass. Before I could come to an answer, and long before I expected to, I fell asleep as well. On that night and many nights to come, I would find it easier to fall asleep with her in my arms than I did on my own.

The next morning, we woke up together, and after a brief snuggle she gave me a big smile and a kiss and thanked me for letting her stay over. She picked up her things and ran out the door, already late for work, and I wondered what had just happened. Given our history, I didn't know if that would be the only time she would stay over, but had a sense that it wouldn't help to text her and ask her to spend more time. I had to let her find her own path to me.

My intuition proved to be right; as the weeks went by she texted and called me more and more often, and before long she was spending at least a night a week at my place. There was a silliness and playfulness to her that would bring out the same in me, a joy and lightness I had not felt in my heart for a long time. Whether we were doing art together, having frozen yogurt, or just walking about exploring the city hand in hand, we would be smiling and laughing the entire time.

Back at my place we would kiss and caress each other passionately while we were in the living room, but the bedroom was only for cuddling, comfort, and sleep. Having been single for a while at that point, I was fine with this – I loved being close to her and sleeping with her always put me in a better mood. I wondered whether this might be my first intimate relationship without sex, and decided that as long as it meant having the closeness and intimacy I craved, I was fine with it.

After a dozen or so nights at my place she asked me to her place for dinner, and as we were cooking she unexpectedly asked me to stay over. Staying at someone else's place always gives me some anxiety, and in this case it was all the greater since she lived with her father. To make matters worse, his room was just across the hall from hers, but as our relationship was non-sexual I reassured myself that it wouldn't be an issue.

She got a toothbrush for me and we got into bed together, getting completely naked. We had been doing this more and more often so that we could feel the closeness of full body contact while we slept. Just as we snuggled up together she whispered to me, "Su, can I put your penis in my mouth?"

I was very surprised, but gladly nodded.

"Okay," she said with a giggle, "But we have to be quiet."

She pulled the covers back, stroking, licking, and sucking me passionately until I came with an intense orgasm; she climbed back up to me to kiss me deeply.

"Can I taste you too?" I asked. I loved giving oral to my partners; to me it has always felt more intimate and personal than penetrative sex and an important step in getting closer with someone.

To my disappointment, she nodded her head "no" vigorously. "Not tonight," she said, "but later." She gave me a little smile, drew my arms around her, pushed herself into the cavity of my torso as she had on so many other nights, falling instantly to sleep.

After that night she told me how she rarely felt sexual desire, and mostly just wanted cuddling, but when she did feel the need arise, it was sudden and intense. This proved to be accurate – I would follow her lead on this, and while we would only have sex once every few months, those times were always powerful and memorable. The very first time her desire arose while we were at my place, she wanted to talk about the things that made me excited. Having learned from the Gabrielle experience how pointless it was to hide the full tapestry of my desires, I started talking about how in addition to vaginal sex I enjoyed having my bottom stimulated, and started talking about my toys.

"I wanna see!" she said, her eyes lighting up. She looked carefully through my collection, and asked "do you have a strap-on, Su?"

"I do," I said nervously.

"You DO?" she asked, even more excited, "Can we use it?"

I laughed happily at how excited she was: this was a very good sign. "Sure!" I said enthusiastically.

We fit it to her body with one of my favorite dildos, and I started getting into my usual position with my head on the pillow. "But I wanna see your pretty face, Su," she said, frowning.

"Oh, ok, we can do it the other way," I said.

I turned around to face her, pulled my legs up towards my body, and helped her guide the dildo into me. Her eyes lit up as she saw it enter further and further into my body.

"Oh, Su," she said with a big smile. I had never seen her this turned on.

Pajamas

She drove the dildo in and out slowly but firmly, with long strokes, coaxing out my inadvertent vocalizations, which turned her on even more. She held on to my hips, watching my face with a huge smile across her lips. Eventually I asked her to put some lube on my cock, and she happily complied, driving the dildo in as she stroked me to a powerful orgasm. The dildo still inside me, she reached down to give me a long, passionate kiss.

"Oh, Su," she said again, before she gently pulled out so we could clean ourselves off.

As we lay in bed together afterwards, I held her close, thrilled at the level of intense physical intimacy we had reached; I was happy with our emotional bonding and cuddling, but this made things even more special. In a moment of vulnerability, I asked, "Why do you even like me, Casey?"

"Why would you say that?" she asked crossly, "Of course I like you. I like you because you're sweet, and you're funny, and because of the pajamas song."

I laughed as I remembered, "Oh yeah, the pajamas song!"

The first time we'd met, more than a decade ago when she was dating my friend Sam, she had come over with him on a night when they were both bored. We got into a long conversation about pajamas, and out of nowhere I started singing "Pajamas" to the tune of Bob Marley's "We're Jamming:"

A Boy Named Su

Pajamas

Pajamas

I want to wear pajamas with you...

Pajamas (pajamas pajamas pajamas)

Pajamas (pajamas pajamas pajamas)

I hope you like Pajamas too...

We started singing it together again and broke off laughing. After a moment, I continued with my questions.

"Okay, those are good reasons, especially the pajamas song, but I mean, you date several other guys, and I'm not at all like them – why do you like me?"

She thought to herself for a second. "Well you know," she said, "I've always been bi, and just before I started dating you I realized I was dating three boys and no girls and so I should really start dating a girl. And then I started dating you, and it was perfect, because it's like dating a boy and a girl at the same time!"

She could not have given a more perfect answer. I was thrilled, hugged and kissed her, and went to sleep with her gathered snugly in my arms, a stuffed animal gathered in hers.

Pajamas

In those early days I was happy with whatever time I could get with Casey, and given how many other people she was dating I knew it would always be limited. As our emotional and physical intimacy grew, however, I unknowingly became more and more dependent on her presence. I remember the precise moment that I realized I had fallen in love with her – she was house-sitting for a neighbor, and she asked me to spend the weekend with her at their charming little house, complete with a friendly pup. We woke up together in each other's arms on Saturday morning, snuggled for a while, went downstairs in our pajamas to make some breakfast, and then had a cup of coffee together.

Sitting there, not saying a word, seeing her smiling eyes over that cup of coffee, I knew. This is what I wanted, this is the person I wanted, this is the life I wanted. While some part of me of course knew this was not our house, and this could never be the monogamous long-term relationship I wanted, I let myself live inside the fantasy for a moment.

With Casey, the ordinary became extraordinary. We would meet up early in the morning and decide to take a ferry to the San Juan Islands; she would delight in all the strange history of the vessel, take me to see all of the boat's features, explore all the decks, and meet all the other travelers, a whole storybook of adventures before we even reached the islands. I would walk a step behind, a huge smile on my face, every moment with her a treasure. Another time we would go on a rainy winter adventure to Bainbridge to see a local resident's festival of Christmas lights, then drive to Tacoma to see their lights in the zoo, finally checking into a downtown hotel, bringing each other to orgasm in the glow of our sister city.

A year after our first summer kiss, we went back to the same summer camping festival. Nestled in a hammock between towering pines hundreds of years older than us, I finally gathered up the courage to tell her I loved her, when she surprised me by pre-empting me with, "Oh Su, I love you," nestling herself into my body. As always, Casey was one step ahead of me, leading us into a new adventure.

In those days we spent at least two nights a week together, often more. She was having some issues with both of the other men she had been seeing most regularly, and I began to secretly hope that perhaps she would consider a monogamous relationship with me. As the year ended, we went to my company holiday party together, and I told her on the way home that even though she wanted me to see other people, I just wanted to see her. She was quiet for a moment.

"That's fine, Su, you don't have to date anyone else if you don't want to. It's just that I care about you, and feel like I won't be available enough to fulfil all of your emotional needs." She was completely right, and I knew she was right, but I didn't want to believe it.

Pajamas

Within months, a new figure entered her dating life, and without warning he started to take up most of her time. From several times a week we dropped to seeing each other once a week; by the next summer one of her other boyfriends had left the picture because of her lack of availability, and she tearfully asked me if it would be OK if we could see each other only once every two weeks. I accepted it, knowing it was not going to be enough for me but also not willing to let her go. Over time, two weeks became three, and even that would only happen if I repeatedly texted to try and find a time. It became more and more clear that if I didn't push for it, we wouldn't end up seeing each other at all. I would crave her presence the many nights she wasn't with me, and began going to bed with a body pillow so I'd have something to hold as I went to sleep.

I held on like this for another year, and eventually I pulled back on contacting her, waiting to see if perhaps she would start reaching out again. Weeks and then a month went by, and finally she scheduled a date. When we met that night, I told her I just couldn't do it anymore; it was tearing me apart, and as she had warned me long ago I wanted much more of her time than she could give.

"OK, Su, if that's the way you feel," she said calmly. There was no malice in her voice, but also less emotion than I had hoped for given the intensity we'd had at our peak. She gave me a long, last hug, and said, "I'm gonna go, Su," and left.

There will always be a warm place in my heart for Casey. She had warned me long before that night that she would not be enough for my heart, and I couldn't blame her for my fooling myself into a fantasy that things might be different. The intensity of our emotional and physical connection is something I'll always treasure. But perhaps more than anything else, she represented my first relationship in which I was really honest about who I was and could truly be myself. She had completely embraced that honest version of me, emotionally and physically. This particular relationship may not have worked out, and I grieved for it, but it did give me hope that I could express my full self and still find the love that I so desperately wanted.

The Second Time Around

Against my better judgment, I was drunk-swiping on tinder on a Friday night, still tipsy after coming home from a happy hour. I've never been very effective at flirting online, so I have always viewed it mostly as entertainment; still, the hope always remains that I might match with someone interesting. Swiping left, left, left, I was surprised to suddenly see Sabine. I paused, swiping neither left nor right, again and again flipping through her photos. She hadn't been single in a longtime, and the last time we had interacted, we had shared a brief kiss before she quickly pulled away. She had been poly, but her previous partner insisted on maintaining tight controls over who she could and could not see. Suddenly, it seemed, she was available again.

I kept looking at her profile and reading her text, focused on one word in her self-description: "dominant." What did she mean by that? Did it mean what I hope it meant? I still had her number in my phone, and sent her a quick text: "Hi

Sabine, how are you? Want to get together for drinks some-time? It's been forever!" I quickly put my phone away, unsure whether this had been a good idea, but it was too late to decide now.

Within moments I saw a response. "I would love to! How about tonight? I'm nearby, want to get dinner with me?"

I was far drunker than I would have wanted to be for a reunion with the quick-witted Sabine, and thought about asking to postpone, but instead decided to just be honest. "Well, I would love to, but I'm already a little tipsy, if that's OK – if not we can find another night!"

"Oh, that's quite all right with me" Sabine wrote back with a smiley emoji. We decided to meet at Artusi, a local favorite of both of ours, in half an hour. I quickly got dressed again, fixed my hair, and headed out the door.

I had met Sabine more than a decade ago, shortly after my experience with Zakai. I had made a profile on a fetish site, speaking of my physical interests in abstract terms such as "being switchy" and using phrases like "I enjoy exploring the full spectrum of sexual roles" rather than explicitly talking about what I was looking for. I posted some photos of my body with my face in shadow, including the one I had posted to Craigslist with my bottom in the air. Though it was not a dating site per se, Sabine had messaged me, and we started a conversation without getting into any detail about sexuality.

Eventually we met for a date, which she would later tell me was the first time someone took her to a nice restaurant for dinner. While we enjoyed each other's company that evening, she told me during dinner that she was still living with her partner. Despite her no longer being sexual with him, I didn't want to enter into the complexity of that situation. At the end of the night, I walked her to her bus stop and waited with her, holding my small umbrella over both of our tiny bodies.

As her bus arrived, looking down at the curb, she said, "I want you to know I find you really attractive."

"I find you really attractive as well," I said sincerely. She looked up at me, smiled briefly and got onto the bus.

A year later I would see her again at a summer festival: in a night filled with swirling lights, loud music, and curious hands, we ended up in the same tent together. For the next few weeks we would see each other regularly, but despite our strong attraction for each other our sexual chemistry never seemed to catch fire. We would have dinner, go to bed, engage in sex that was pleasurable but devoid of real passion, and she would leave quietly in the morning.

It was around this time that Gabrielle and I finally started dating after a year of meeting and flirting. When that began to feel serious, I told Sabine that I really wanted to try and focus on a monogamous relationship with Gabi. Since Sabine insisted on being polyamorous, this wasn't even an option with her. I remember she had a slight head cold the night I told her; in between sniffles, she rolled her eyes and said, "good luck with that." I realized she was disappointed, but wasn't sure what else to say.

In the years since then, we had seen each other at parties and gatherings many times, and always felt the same strong attraction to each other. More than once, without intending to, we would end up making out at these parties on a couch or in a dark corner, but it would go no further, even when we were both single; we both remembered what had happened the previous time and resolved to appreciate each other at a distance.

Tonight, though, a decade after that first meeting, things felt somehow different. It was the first time we had met each other one-on-one since those nights together, and our conversation and laughter were clicking as they had in our best of times. We kept ordering drinks, laughing and talking and flirting as the night went on. At some point I began to feel the drinks from dinner and from earlier accumulating.

"Okay," I said, "so I'm getting pretty drunk, and I think I need to go home. It's totally cool if you want to call it a night, but if you want to come with me, we could hang out there."

The Second Time Around

A big smile crossed her face. "Yes, let's go to your place! I have a date later, but not until midnight."

"Perfect," I smiled, and shortly we were on our way.

My place was ten or so blocks away and we decided to walk. The crisp November air felt refreshing on our skin after the warm evening of drinks, and we huddled together a bit on the way. We stood a little apart from each other in the elevator, stealing looks and giggling, and I still wasn't entirely sure what was going to happen next.

As soon as we entered my place, all the uncertainty fell away. She grabbed me in an intense kiss, and I fumbled to close and lock the door with my other hand. We stayed like that in the kitchen, our arms around each other, her kisses hungry and passionate, stronger and more confident than they had been all those years ago.

We started taking off each other's coats and she pulled her face slightly away from me to speak. With rapid breath she said quietly but firmly, "I want sex – can we have sex?"

It was incredibly sexy to hear this from her, and I quickly nodded and said "yes."

We walked into my bedroom and started taking off the rest of our clothes, kneeling in front of each other on the bed as we kissed. Given my recent experiences and what had motivated me to contact her tonight, I knew I had to open my mouth now or be forever filled with regret. I pulled away from her lips to say, "Um, so, I noticed on your tinder profile that it said you enjoyed being dominant. Does that mean you, er, like strap-ons?" My drunkenness was making me more direct than usual.

Her face once again broke into a huge smile. "Oh YES!" she said, and kissed me hard, then pulled away, a sly smirk on her face. "Wait a minute, is that why you contacted me, because you saw me on tinder?"

I suddenly blushed, "uh, well, I just thought..."

She laughed, "it's fine, I think it's cute, I'm really glad you texted me. So, do you have a strap-on?"

"Oh yeah!" I said, excited to show her my toys.

We fit the harness around her body, and while I pointed to the green dildo I usually had my lovers use, she asked if she could use a purple one that was shaped much more like an erect cock. I had never been fucked with that one before, but she was looking at it longingly, and I was excited to see her so excited.

As we pulled the straps tight, she remarked at how much better of a fit this harness was than others she had tried. She started stroking the shaft of her new appendage, saying, "wow, this really feels like having a cock!" I took the rest of my clothes off and started stroking the cock with my hand on hers, which was really turning her on. Caught up in the moment, I reached down and put my lips around it, something I had never done before.

"Wow that's really hot," she said, breathing harder now, and thrusting gently into my mouth. "Okay my turn," she said, a confident smile on her face, pushing my shoulder down onto the bed and lifting my legs into the air.

Despite being smaller than me, she was strong, and I was very willing. She started rubbing lube into my bottom and gently eased the head of the stiff cock inside me, then started firmly stroking in and out. Much firmer and more curved towards her body, this cock was an entirely different feel than the one I'd used in strap-ons before, and I made a mental note to try out the others from my collection as well.

As the inadvertent "mmm" sounds started to come out of me, she became even more turned on.

"Oh, I love the sounds you're making," she said with a smile.

She held onto my legs and then my torso, alternating between fucking me hard and then pausing while fully inside me, reaching down to kiss me. She was really into it in a way I hadn't seen since Stacey, and her intensity was turning me on more and more. Eventually I couldn't wait any longer, and asked between breaths if she could lube up my cock.

"Oh, of course," she said, again with a sly smile. She started stroking it but with a teasing softness, increasing the intensity with a deliciously excruciating slowness.

Finally, just when I thought I could take no more, I exploded in a powerful orgasm that left us both gasping for breath. We grinned broadly at each other, a glistening layer of sweat coating both our bodies.

"That was SO hot," she said.

"Oh my god yes," I said. "And to think of all those times we were together back then and we never tried this!"

"I know, right?" she said, and we both laughed. "I think we have to do this more regularly," she continued, and I nodded vigorously in agreement.

Over the next few weeks we did see each other frequently, meeting up for an art opening or dinner and then heading back for an intense night of sex. Some nights she would wear the strap-on; others I would be the one putting on the condom, but everything we tried had a level of intensity we'd never experienced in our past encounters.

Unfortunately, both of us were in periods of rapid change in other parts of our lives, and after a while it became harder and harder for us to schedule time together. We would text and plan for some future night but at some point she asked if we could put things on pause while she figured out some career issues that needed her full attention. Our connection was more physical than emotional, so I was happy to give her the time she needed, and we both assumed that later on we would return to our intense nights of passion.

Life has a habit of getting in the way, though, and by the time one of us had more time, the other didn't, and within a few months both of us had entered into other relationships. We remain close friends to this day, and I often think of the experience as an important piece of "evidence." In science, the most meaningful evidence comes from A/B tests, where we manipulate one variable between values A and B while keeping everything else as equal as possible. For example, to test the effectiveness of a drug (A) vs. a placebo (B), we try to find two groups of people who are equivalent in all other ways, assigning one to each condition and then measuring the results.

My two experiences with Sabine, separated by a space of a decade, form the closest thing to a controlled experiment I can point to with respect to hiding my true self (A) vs. being open and vulnerable (B). The resulting effect on our sexual intimacy could not be more dramatic: when I tried to play the "regular guy" in condition A, our sex was boring and passionless; when

I revealed my desire for her to fuck me (B), it was intense and incredible, no matter who was on top.

Since then, every time I consider playing it safe and trying to be that "regular guy" when flirting with someone, I think back to Sabine, and remember how much more is possible if only I'm willing to ask for it. Rather than focusing on the negatives of what might happen if I do reveal my true self, embarrassing as they might be, I find myself thinking about what I could be missing out on if I don't. Besides, who am I to ignore the laws of science?

Spider Gwen in Therapy

"No, not Spider-*Man*, Spider *Gwen*. She appears in this movie, *Into the Spiderverse*, where there are multiple characters with Spider-Man-like powers that come from alternate universes. Anyway, that's not really important. Someone at this party was wearing this costume, and she looked incredible and sexy dancing in it. Or maybe not *she*, that's my point. I couldn't be sure whether it was a she or a he; they were slender and athletic so it was hard to say for sure, though the way they were dancing and moving made them seem very feminine. That's when I realized *I* could wear that costume, and nobody would know whether I was a woman or a man either!"

Across from me, Matthew smiled and nodded, as he always did, preparing to ask a question. Matthew is my therapist of some years now, a kindly, older man who has been immensely helpful in making me think through my identity and desires, mostly by making me face the things that I would much prefer to keep hidden beneath an avalanche of distractions. Still, at this moment, he frustrates me for not immediately understanding exactly what I feel inside, which I recognize is grossly unfair, since I don't understand it myself.

"So you would wear this costume and people would think you were a woman?" he asks.

"No," I said, frustrated, "they *wouldn't know*, that's the point."

"Okay," said Matthew calmly, never flustered by my frustration, "and then you would meet women in that costume?"

"Something like that, yes," I said, unsure of what I really would do at that point. "I mean, I feel like if they didn't know, they would see me differently, and they would want to interact with me, even if ordinarily they would only be interested in other women."

Matthew took a drink from his ever-present water bottle and shifted in his chair. "And what would you tell them?"

"I... I don't know," I responded, now frustrated with myself, "I mean, I wouldn't want to *mislead* them, I just want them to *see* me as I really am before they start making a lot of assumptions about who I am."

As always, Matthew was raising the right questions. What *would* I tell them? That under the Spider Gwen costume, there was a male costume of flesh and blood, and under that costume was a really complex distribution that spanned the gender spectrum?

In my ordinary skin and clothes, women I meet are often confused about where I'm coming from; it is such a common experience I've learned to read it in their faces. Most of the time, as soon as I start talking to a woman, they see that I am not the usual cis het man they expect, and without other information they quickly revert to the binary and assume that I am gay. Men are less subtle about their reactions but tend have the same impression – I always get a ton of attention from gay men, which I find flattering and delightful, despite having to smilingly turn down their advances. Many straight male friends are so certain I'm gay they've tried to introduce me to potential lovers; my favorite is my dear friend Ralphie who at no less than five different parties has pulled me aside to delicately (he thinks) broach the question.

"Look, Su, I know you're gay..." he begins.

"I'm not though," I respond, smiling.

"Yeah, sure, but you're bi though," he continues, his words slurring a bit, at this point already obviously drunk, as we've had this conversation many times before.

"Actually, not really; I pretty much exclusively date women, though I have been with a guy before," I continue.

"Wait, really?" he says, pulling back, always surprised at this point. "But you date guys sometimes, right?"

"Not really..." at this point I'm laughing, and have to explain to him how many times we've been through this.

This does not bother me at all in itself – I know many people at work assume I am gay, and I am happy to let them continue believing that, rather than having a long and difficult discussion about my gender identity that they would struggle to understand. The problem, though, is when this impression occurs in women I am interested in – they then assume that I have no romantic interest in them, so the flirtation is done before it even begins.

There have been various exceptions over the years; women who ordinarily date other women but end up flirting or making out with me, always surprised at themselves afterwards but sensing something in me at the moment that they can't explain. Most of the women I've dated and certainly all of those with whom I've had strong chemistry have been bisexual; it's not surprising that given their broad range of attraction, they would be the ones best able to recognize and appreciate the full gender spectrum within me. Still, I feel like many opportunities are lost when I am trying to flirt with someone who might be interested or even excited about my gender identity, yet I don't say anything. They make their assumptions, I play my expected role, and of course nothing happens, time and time again.

"Why don't you just tell them?" Matthew asks.

"Well..." I hesitate, "I mean, that might turn them off if that's the first thing I say."

Matthew sits up in his chair, "Well if it turns them off then it's probably not going to work out anyway!" he says incredulously.

"Well, maybe, but maybe they would want to date me thinking I was just a regular guy, and I don't want to miss out on that possibility," I say ruefully.

"But what happens three weeks or three months down the road when they get to know you?" Matthew continues.

"Well, I'm pretty good at hiding that part of myself," I respond, shifting uncomfortably on his couch.

"And how has that worked out for you," he says with friendly sarcasm, throwing up his hands up in the air.

"Er... not well?" I laugh, and he laughs with me.

He is right of course, and increasingly I am willing to be more forward about my true self, as I know all too well the consequences of trying to hide it. There is still a part of me that doesn't want to restrict the set of possible partners to those who are comfortable with my genderqueerness, but after years of Matthew's gentle (and sometimes sarcastic) prodding, I've come to recognize how ridiculous it is to even consider a relationship with someone who doesn't appreciate the whole of me. For many years, though, the thought someone loving me for who I am felt so far outside the realm of possibility, that I couldn't even take it seriously. Covering up that part of myself felt like the only option.

As I became more convinced that I needed to talk about it, I came up against a new challenge – what exactly should I say? I started out thinking about bringing up how I liked pegging (or the general category of "butt stuff," as we say colloquially in Seattle), but it felt uncomfortably intimate for a first conversation.

"I can't just walk up to someone and say, 'Hi, I'm Su, and I like butt stuff,'" I blurted out in one of our sessions. Even Matthew laughed out loud at that one.

I also began to realize this approach was overly focused on physicality and sex. I felt amazingly loved and appreciated by Casey despite the fact that we only had strap-on sex that one time; it was that she *saw* me as I truly was and loved me for it ("it's like dating a boy and a girl at the same time!" she had said).

Over the years of working with Matthew, I've begun to shift my language to talk more about gender rather than sex. For a while I toyed with the term genderfluid, but that seemed not quite right for me, as it was often used in the context of fashion and appearance, and the whole challenge was expressing what was going on *underneath* my skin. I briefly referred to myself as "genderweird," though that felt self-deprecating and off the mark as well. Initially, I had steered away from the term "genderqueer" because it felt like avoiding the question, as though I were checking the "it's complicated" option in the gender box. It took me a few years to realize that this was, in fact, exactly how I felt, and finally I embraced the term as my own.

The most common reaction I now get to saying I'm genderqueer is a surprised, "Oh, I didn't know that, what pronouns should I use for you?" I appreciate the caring inherent to this response, in their wanting to refer to me in the way I would prefer, but I find it an unsatisfying reaction if that's as far as it goes. I tell these well-meaning friends that I'm completely comfortable with my male costume and that he/him pronouns are fine; it's only with people I'm intimate with that this identity really matters. This is only partially true, as I do still want these friends to know – mostly in the hopes that they might eventually see the real me.

The reaction I wish for, and only rarely encounter, whether it's a friend or someone I'm flirting with, is the friendly smile and a follow-up of curious questions. "What does that mean for you?" This is the stage, though, where I often start to stammer today. It's still hard for me to succinctly explain, and I try to instead tell stories that illustrate where I fall on the gender spectrum. As I'm still nervous just to have this conversation, I tilt the stories towards what I call the "cool guy" version, where I don't display the full vulnerability I feel, and end up sounding like I'm bragging about past lovers, which is of course not my intent at all (not to mention a huge turn-off).

"Maybe I should just write it all down," I say with exasperation to Matthew. "Write down all those stories, the vulnerable versions, and just hand them to someone, and say, 'here, read this.' Like an user manual for dating Su. I really don't know how else to explain it."

He looks concerned. "Well, work with me here," he says, the phrase I've come to recognize as his signal for me to slow down and really think about what I'm saying, "why do you think you need to do all that?"

"I mean, how else are they every going to understand what's really going on inside me?" I ask.

"Why not try, I don't know, talking to them?" he asks, semi-sarcastically.

"How would even do that?" I shot back.

He sits up in his chair again, "Well of course you're not going to get it right the first time, but don't you think you would get better at it if you started trying?"

"I don't know…" I trail off, already thinking about the book – this book – in my mind, writing down the stories, sharing it with people. Suddenly I'm imagining a future where the book is released and has become unexpectedly popular. "Oh! And if I did write that book and it somehow was a hit, maybe at a reading I would be able to meet someone who really understood me," I blurt out, getting completely lost in my dream at this point.

"Or maybe," Matthew says slowly, "you don't need to do *any* of that."

"Huh?" I say, shaken out of my dream.

"What if you're enough just as you are?" he asks quietly.

"What do you mean?" I asked, genuinely not understanding.

He repeats himself, more slowly, "What if… you're *enough*… just as you are?"

"Yeah…" I say, sinking back into the chair, wanting to believe it, but not believing it, thinking I might be able to believe it, but not believing it.

Yet.

A Boy Named Su

The Girl You'll Never Know

"OK, let me ask you something about all this *gender* stuff," Richard interrupted.

He leaned into the table, surprising me, as I had just started telling him about what it meant for me to be genderqueer. I had expected him to at least wait to hear what I had to say; apparently, I had expected too much.

"A few months ago, this actress Debra Messing posted a photo of 'erotic' cupcakes with frosting vaginas on them to celebrate International Women's Day, yeah? It was cute and a lot of people seemed to like it, she got tons of positive comments. Then some *trans* women," he continued, rolling his eyes and with an ugly emphasis on the word, "started complaining about how this excluded women who didn't have vaginas, and she had to apologize. What do you think of that?"

From his tone, it was pretty clear what *he* thought of that, and it made me wince. Still, I had known Richard for a long time, and was mostly accustomed to his brusque manner getting on my nerves from time to time. I tried my best to keep my doubts in check and assume good intent.

"Well, I think it's important that they brought it up, and I'm glad to hear she apologized instead of doubling down," I responded, as calmly as I could.

Richard had a skeptical frown on his face, and was about to start speaking again, but this time I was the one who interrupted, attempting to make it more personal with a story of my own.

"So, I had a similar experience a few years ago. I had participated in the women's march, and posted a photo of a popular signboard, featuring a vagina and a clever slogan. The photo got a lot of likes, but a friend who is trans wrote to me and told me how it was hurtful and exclusionary, and how many women like her feel marginalized on International Women's Day. My immediate reaction on seeing her message was defensive, but once I thought it through, I felt terrible that I had not considered that perspective. I apologized to her, took down the photo, and put up a note in its place explaining why it had been problematic."

Richard was unconvinced. "Yeah but is that really the most important thing to worry about, I mean..." he said with a snicker before I interrupted him again.

With the snicker my shields went up; I then engaged in the hopeless dance of trying to rationally convince someone out of a bias they have no rational basis for.

"Yes, it *is* important," I continued, "and we don't have to focus on only one thing. We can do both: we can celebrate International Women's Day while still including trans women."

He made a face and changed the subject, never returning to ask about my being genderqueer. At this point, though, I was relieved; it no longer felt *safe* to talk to him about it, and I was glad to have found out before sharing something that vulnerable. I silently realized I would probably never talk to him about this topic. Still, I don't hold it against him: so few people do end up being safe, I've become accustomed to this kind of response.

Safety is something that all of us the gender spectrum think about constantly. According to the National Center for Transgender Equality, in 2020 more than one in four trans people have been the victim of a bias-driven assault, and these rates are even higher for trans women vs. trans men. But even those statistics are just the tip of the iceberg, counting only those events egregious enough to warrant police reports and press attention. In everyday conversation, discussions of gender and gender identity often provoke the snickers I heard from Richard, if not outright defensiveness about "redefining womanhood" or false narratives about how transgender rights would somehow result in a rash of men attacking women in bathrooms.

Trans women were at the forefront of the Stonewall uprising against police brutality towards LGBTQIA+ people in 1969. But as we learn in David France's heartbreaking documentary, *The Death and Life of Marsha P. Johnson*, they were quickly sidelined in the larger movement. While North American culture seems to be slowly but increasingly accepting of the "LG" part of LGBTQIA+, the rest of the letters seem to have been left behind. The once one-dimensional gender binary has now become a two-dimensional binary of biological sex and sexual preference: in polite society, one can be (one of) male or female and (one of) straight or gay.

The reality, of course, is not this two-dimensional view, but something more like a four-dimensional gender hypercube, where the third axis is gender *identity*. This dimension is still difficult for most people to accept, understand, or empathize with. The fourth axis is gender expression, the way we choose to dress and carry ourselves in the world. I'm sure there are also fifth and sixth axes I am missing; we're still just beginning to develop the language to meaningfully discuss the full complexity of gender.

What makes things even more complicated is that any person can have a distribution along *any* of these axes — consider a particular intersex individual, who has a distribution along the dimension of biological sex, happens to have a clear gender identity of male, and is sexually attracted to both men and women. Perhaps due to my surgery, I too am a distribution on the biological axis, lacking in body hair and unusually soft of skin. I'm also very much a distribution on the axis of gender identity. My sexual preference, though, is very strongly biased towards women, and my gender expression – my daily costume – is unequivocally male.

In a world where safety was not a concern, perhaps I would choose a broader range for gender expression as well. Perhaps I (and many others) would dress and carry ourselves across the gender spectrum in a context-dependent way. In such a world I could slip on a female costume as easily and well as I do my male skin, and I would do so whenever the mood struck me, going home to change back into my male costume before an evening date (or not, depending on the date). Male business suit by day, gender-ambiguous sprite at the bar with my friends, Spider Gwen at the dance party – the possibilities are endless. I'd have to budget for at least twice the number of clothes and shoes, and it would be well worth the expense.

But that, however, is not the world we live in, so instead I hide inside my male costume most of the time. I've grown comfortably aware of its privilege in various settings – I am never accosted in the street (though I do often hear harmless flirty callouts from gay men), I am always listened to in meetings, I am never talked down to at the auto shop. In most scenarios, this doesn't bother me; like Bowie in *the Man Who Fell to Earth*, I am wholly aware it is a costume, and roll my eyes to myself as people make their assumptions and treat me according to their archaic mental models.

Don't get me wrong – there are also aspects of my male body that I adore – I love having a penis, both for masturbation and for entering into welcoming bodies, I love the feeling of an intense orgasm coursing through my veins, I love the way my muscles look when I've been working out, I love the way the sweat glistens off my skin after exertion, I love the smell of my body and its surprising strength despite my small size.

In the presence of someone I'm attracted to, though, this all breaks down. I want them to see the whole of my identity, to be drawn or repelled based on my entire being and not just my outer shell. As such, I am willing to make a slight opening in the costume here and there, showing a bit of the alien skin underneath, knowing the damage it could sustain but risking it for the opportunity to make a real connection. Sometimes I do this by telling a story, sometimes it's by a careful response to a question. Sometimes under the influence I'm a little more direct, but most of the time, I'm quick to go back to the safety of my shell.

I remember a recent party where I saw a beautiful woman with iridescent skin even darker than my own, animatedly gesturing with her hands to a group of friends. I pushed through my usual shyness to go with sit with the group and they generously included me in their conversation. Out of the blue, the woman who had drawn me in suddenly sat up. She had noticed a massage table where some clever person had fit an orbital sander with an extra fluffy cover and was rubbing it over people's bodies, eliciting squeals of delight.

"I want to try that," she said, "does anyone want to do it with me?" and looked right at me.

"I'd be happy to," I said quickly, blushing.

I was more than willing to massage her beautiful skin with the vibrating device, and afterwards she did the same for me. I was surprised and a little embarrassed to hear the inadvertent "mmm" sounds coming out of me, but she didn't seem to mind at all.

As I got down from the table, she excitedly said, "I wonder what else they have at this party."

"Yeah!" I said, "I know they have a bondage rope setup upstairs, but that's not really my thing."

Looking directly at me with her intense, dark eyes, she asked, "So what *is* your thing?"

I froze like a deer in headlights. "Um, uh, I like all kinds of things, like, uh, all sides of the equation, you know," I stammered.

"Uh-huh," she said as she turned to look around, clearly unimpressed by my answer. "Let's just go upstairs and dance," she said, and I meekly followed, feeling like I just missed out on a golden opportunity.

"Why didn't you say, 'I LOVE BUTT SEX!'" my therapist Matthew yelled at me when I told him this story, and we both had a good laugh.

"That's probably what I should have done," I said ruefully.

"Let's be real here," Matthew said, the tell-tale sign that a challenging question was coming next. "Would a more *fully empowered* Su have said that to her?"

I shifted uncomfortably in my chair, realizing how much further I still had to go. "Yeah..." I mumbled.

I would certainly like to be unconditionally out and proud, not only with potential lovers but also in my everyday life, yet the realities of my daily interactions always give me pause. In a recent conversation with another friend about being genderqueer, I remember her saying, "Huh, I don't know anyone else who's trans or genderqueer," which quickly dampened my enthusiasm. It's not that you don't know anyone, I thought to myself, mentally noting several genderqueer friends we had in common – it's that they don't feel safe talking to you about it. It reminded me of when my male friends say (shockingly often), "I don't know anyone personally that has had an abortion," whereas that's statistically almost impossible in most of my circles. Once again, it's because those mutual friends didn't feel safe telling this person about their experiences. As a result, while I am increasingly trying to risk vulnerability for someone I'm attracted to (though even then only if I sense an opening), my threshold is very high for friends or colleagues, and the slightest hint of danger will make me shy away from saying more.

I'd ask you to think about this for a moment: if your reaction to the above is "that's fine, I'd rather not know," so be it. Your actions are likely consistent with your desires, and honestly it's what we expect from most people. But if you do sincerely want to know people like me, I'd advise you to make an effort to create psychological safety. Those of us who are struggling with the way society treats our identities are hyper-sensitive to any signs of danger, and will shrink away at the smallest of red flags. Our antennae are always up, listening for jokes, watching for smirks, decoding reactions to news stories, and the like.

That said, we are also very forgiving of mistakes if it's clear there is good intent and a genuine curiosity to learn. If you reach out and ask us about our experiences, ask us *why* we've chosen these words to describe ourselves and what they *mean* to us, listen to us and ask us questions without judgment, and over time support us in our true identity, we will be overjoyed to bring you closer into our lives. There is nothing we would love more than to be fully accepted by even one more person, to know we could truly be ourselves with you, to make our worlds that much less lonely. We would love to explain the perspectives from which we see the world, how ordinary experiences for you may feel very different to us, how the journey of becoming who we truly are is both terrifying and life-affirming.

As a last thought, I'd like to remind you that for each of us on this gender spectrum, there is a sea of stories far beyond the few I've told in this book. As our friends, colleagues, and lovers, you know our shores, our tastefully decorated waterfronts, the calm currents and distant storms on our surface; wouldn't you also like to know the depths that roil below?

We will watch anxiously if you start to tiptoe along the wet sand, taking those first tentative steps into our waters. Take your time: the waves are endless, and if you enter with gentleness and let the water carry you, we will gladly support you in your journey. In that moment, you will see our eyes widen and our arms open, the crest of a wave rushing to meet you in a soft crash of joy.

The Girl You'll Never Know

We have been waiting for you.

A Boy Named Su

Acknowledgements

This book would not have come together without the encouragement of many people dear to my heart.

First I must thank my literary hero, Roxane Gay, whose incredible books exploring complex issues via personal narratives have been my inspiration and guide. Your work has been my north star throughout this process.

I'd also like to thank the friends, lovers, and partners who adorn these pages as well as the halls of my memories. Each of you has been a teacher to me, and without you, there would have been no stories to tell. A warm nod also to my therapist, "Matthew," without whom I would not have had the perspective or courage to face the truth of many of these tales.

Next, my most heartfelt thanks to all of my early readers, who encouraged me and gave me feedback when this book was in its earliest, rawest stages. Ethan, Keridwyn, Corey, Bethany, Aury, Devon, Selena, Taylor, Liz, Kit, Sarah, and Jill –

knowing you were out there made me keep going, even when I couldn't bear it, editing chapters over and over again to make something worthy of your review.

Finally, to all my LGBTQIA+ readers, I dedicate this book to you. May we all find a path to living our true selves; may we all find a family that accepts us wholly for who we are.

About the Author

Sumu Tasib is a writer, maker, and scientist living in Seattle, Washington. *A Boy Named Su* is his first book, a collection of stories also appearing on Medium under a publication of the same name. Sumu can be found on Medium or Twitter as @sumutasib.

Made in the USA
Columbia, SC
20 September 2021